MEN AFLAME

The Story of the First 30 Years of CBMC/CBMCI

(Formerly Christian Businessmen's Committee International;
Currently Christian Businessmen's Connection)

BY

David R. Enlow

CBMC

Christian Businessmen's Connection
Chattanooga, Tennessee

MEN AFLAME
©2008 CBMC, Inc.
Reprinted 90th Anniversary Edition ©2019 CBMC, Inc.

Originally printed in 1962 by Zondervan Publishing House
Grand Rapids, Michigan

ISBN 978-1-947457-20-1   First paperback edition

Printed in the United States of America

FORWARD

We have reprinted *Men Aflame* as a gift to the men of our CBMC Movement who are dedicated to reaching the men in the marketplace for Christ!

We enjoy a rich Christian heritage in CBMC as seen through the stories in this book. It is filled with the evidence of the Holy Spirit using men to glorify God. They were ordinary businessmen whom God used in remarkable ways, and God can use them again to inspire you and me to be faithful men living everyday to honor our Savior and Lord.

We hope our current generation will be filled with a passion for Christ that will set them aflame like these men were. Please allow the Spirit freedom to work in your life as you read this compelling 30 year era in the history of CBMC.

We are trusting God to elevate your heart to a new pinnacle of desire, that you will want more than ever to be an instrument of hope in the hand of our loving Lord. May your compassion for the lost reach a revived intensity beyond your expectation! Hopefully, current and future generations will stand in awe of Jesus Christ, bearing spiritual fruit for eternity. May our legacy have the same transforming power in their lives as these stories will have in your life as you read this book.

Servants and fellow soldiers by the grace of God

In the early days of the Christian Business Men's Committee movement, I was introduced to an enthusiastic group of witnessing Christian business men in the San Francisco area. I was amazed and thrilled by their intensive zeal for souls. Christ, rather than Christianity, was their motivation.

These laymen confronted men and women with the Gospel in the highways and hedges of the business world. In the midst of full schedules and heavy business responsibilities they retained a sense of spiritual urgency. They were "instant in season" to share their faith with taxi drivers, elevator operators, waitresses and news boys as eagerly as with their business and professional associates. Sweet are the memories of my close friendship and fellowship in the Word with Arnold Grunigen, truly one of God's men aflame, a pioneer and staunch leader of Christian Business Men's Committee International.

During the early 1940's, and following World War II, the Lord used many others in local Christian Business Men's Committees to encourage my heart and strengthen the ministry of the Old Fashioned Revival Hour. I recall instances of human interest and rich fellowship with Christian Business Men's Committees across our land and in Canada, where Premier Manning expressed his personal interest and cooperation.

The Lord used the faithful leadership of local committees spiritually to spark our rallies in Boston Gardens and Chicago's Soldier Field. Also, the Christian Business Men were leaders in planning and praying for the thousands who came to rallies in Cleveland, Toledo, Kansas City, Des Moines, Waterloo, Denver, Seattle, Portland, Oakland—to name several. Some people probably came to these rallies just to see what this radio preacher looked like. Many Christians, I am sure, came and brought unsaved friends because they had confidence in a meeting sponsored by the Christian Business Men's Committee. And the Lord Himself caused many hungry souls to hear and receive the Gospel through these rallies.

No one can measure how much these sponsoring committees did to enlarge the radio audience and build interest in the Revival Hour broadcasts. Also, these Christian laymen, who laid aside denominational labels to advertise and prayerfully to set up each meeting, were the means God used to stir many churches into a man-to-man soul winning ministry and to be a great encouragement to pastors preaching the Word.

God has many methods and men to accomplish His purposes in the world. Eternity alone will reveal the great number of souls in Glory because faithful Christian laymen are diligent in their businesses, fervent in spirit and instant in serving the Lord.

Your heart will be strangely warmed as you read of these *men aflame* whom God has empowered by the Holy Spirit to stand in the gap and make up the hedge. May their story challenge all who read to become men committed to a great God, energetically sharing the joy of their great salvation in Christ.

Dr. Charles E. Fuller
Pasadena, California

CONTENTS

CHAPTER ONE

A BAND OF MEN

". . . and there went with him a band of men, whose hearts God had touched" (I Samuel 10:26).

ON JANUARY 11, 1956, Ralph Edwards and his then popular "This Is Your Life" telecast trained cameras on a handsome young Indianapolis insurance executive. Major Clay Conner had distinguished himself during World War II by organizing the Filipino underground in the hectic days of 1943. He could not tell the whole story in thirty minutes, of course. Left untold at that time was "the most important weekend of my life," a climactic postwar period in 1952.

After the noise of battle had subsided, Conner returned to the States with many scars and much pain. He had seen many men die, some pumped with water until they were bloated and broken apart. Some had starved to death. Many had died of sickness. He hoped to forget what he had seen.

After moving from New York City to Indianapolis in 1948 Conner began to build an insurance agency. One of his first clients was a successful dentist, Dr. Robert K. George, an active member of the Christian Business Men's Committee in Indianapolis.

"I had been tipped off," Conner said, "that Dr. George was somewhat of a religious fanatic. But I resolved to listen to him politely rather than risk offending him. At dinner with me one evening in a public restaurant, he pulled a Bible out of his pocket and began to read. Then he asked me a question: 'Clay, have you ever had a real experience with your Creator?'

"Instead of paying attention to the conversation, I looked to see if anyone was watching this brazen display of religion. To my relief, the food came and I expected the nonsense to end.

"'Don't you think we ought to pray?' Dr. George asked.

"Before I had time to reply, he returned thanks and I died a thousand deaths of embarrassment. During the meal he told me what Jesus Christ had done for him and what He could do for me. It continued until we parted for the evening."

About a month later Dr. George called Clay Conner and invited him to be his guest at a men's retreat in Ohio.

"I'm sorry, Doc," Conner replied, "I'm all booked up this weekend; I couldn't possibly go."

"It's a week from Friday," the dentist continued, "and I've already made reservations. I'll pick you up at two o'clock." And he hung up the receiver.

Clay Conner expressed amusement, then disgust. Dr. George was too good a client to lose, he thought. He would bury his feelings and plan to go with his persistent friend. But what in the world is a retreat? His wife could offer no help on the question.

"The first fellow I met at the retreat," Conner said, "was Art Arthur of Lima, Ohio. He carried a big Bible under his arm and had a disarming smile. 'Isn't it wonderful to be here?' he greeted me. 'I guess so,' I responded quite feebly. Then these men sang hymns far into the night and talked about sharing testimonies.

"This was all completely new to me. I began to wonder whether I was among a group of really rational, sane men, or had they all flipped. But something about their singing impressed me.

"Early in the morning," Conner continued, "after a *beautiful* night's rest on one of those awful double-decker iron bunks, half frozen to death, I was awakened by someone shaking me. 'Get up! Get up!' he said. From the tone of his voice I thought there must be a fire somewhere. 'What's the matter? What's the matter?' I asked, not wanting to be outdone by his fervor and urgency.

"'We're going to prayer meeting,' he said simply.

"'I can hardly wait,' I told him. 'That's just what I came for! You go ahead; I'll see you at breakfast.'

"'Oh, no,' he countered cheerfully. 'Everyone goes to prayer meeting.'"

In the meeting hall, Conner saw men who had gathered from Christian Business Men's Committees in Ohio, Michigan and Indiana. Waldo Yeager, president of the Cortland Produce Company in Toledo, stood before the men. After a few introductory remarks, he said, "now we'll have a season of prayer."

"A season of prayer," thought Clay Conner. "It's September; they'll pray till Christmas!"

Without any signal, the men quickly dropped to their knees. Conner soon found himself standing alone. The kneeling men blocked his path to the door. Conner was trapped. Quietly he, too, knelt on the cold, hard floor. In his discomfort, he heard an earnest intercession.

"Lord," a man was praying, "if there be anyone here with us who doesn't know Jesus Christ, may this be his moment of decision. May he give his life over to Thee."

Conner suddenly felt all alone. "How does that stranger know about my need?" he asked. "All my life culminated right then and there. The terrible events of the past flashed before me. How thankful I was still to be alive. 'Lord,' I prayed silently, 'if You want my life, take it.'"

Clay Conner heard no clanging bells and saw no flashing lights, but he felt a deep inner peace settle on him. The prayers of the men warmed his heart. He forgot the coldness and hardness of the damp concrete as he knelt in prayer. Time seemed to stand still.

In the breakfast line some minutes later, one of the men greeted him. Then he asked, "Are you a Christian?" For a moment the query startled the young insurance executive. Then he replied confidently, "Yes, I am." The questioner continued, "When were you saved?" Conner could hardly believe the sound of his own voice as he responded: "Just a few minutes ago over in the prayer meeting."

A former Detroit and Toledo meat executive, Harry Ernst, heard the conversation. Suddenly he threw his arm around Conner's shoulders. Now inside the mess hall, Ernst shouted, "Meet a new babe in Christ." Tears of joy trickled down his cheeks. Animated conversation followed amid expressions of praise to God.

"Suddenly I realized I was one of them," Conner said. "Minutes earlier I had considered them fanatics and crackpots."

In subsequent weeks, Conner felt he could never find sufficient time to read his Bible. Even with half of his day devoted to insurance and half to searching the Scriptures, he discovered an insatiable thirst and hunger for more knowledge about God and His Son Jesus Christ. To help fill his need, he began a weekly Bible study hour in his home. Soon neighbors and friends heard about the study hour and crowded his home from week to week.

Arriving home late from an important business appointment one evening, on the usual Bible study night, Conner went to the back of his house. A stranger sat in the doorway.

"You'll have to go downstairs and bring up a chair," he said. "The place is crowded out."

The Bible study hour has continued through the years.

Many men and women, and young people as well, have discovered the same kind of faith that came to Clay Conner of Indianapolis. Their discovery was possible partly because Conner had shared his faith with thousands of persons in the quiet of his own home. Thanks to a faithful dentist, and a weekend in Ohio, many lives have been brought from darkness to light.

The retreat which Conner attended is only one of many Christian Business Men's Committee projects and activities geared to confront men with the Gospel of Jesus Christ. Clay Conner is only one man among thousands of men who have received a personal faith in God because of the vision and burden of business and professional men. These men have united in the task of extending the ministry of their local churches. Their task is accomplished by their going out into the "highways and hedges" and compelling others to come in.

CHAPTER TWO

DILIGENT IN BUSINESS

"In my daily calling, make me diligent in business, fervent in spirit, serving the Lord. May I do my work, not for the wages I may get, nor to secure an advance; but so as to please Thee." – F. B. Meyer

WHEN A HANDFUL OF MEN met in Chicago in 1930 to plan an evangelistic campaign, they had no idea of the eventual results of the campaign. On the national scene President Herbert Hoover signed the Hawley-Smoot Tariff as the new decade began.

Internationally, a five-nation Navy pact was signed by the United States, Great Britain, Japan, France and Italy. Depression continued to grip the country.

Evangelical leaders, representing several different organizations, felt the time was ripe for spiritual advance. Surely the nation must feel its need of God now if ever, they thought. Out of their thinking came the first Christian Business Men's Committee—a small band of men in Chicago intent on "redeeming the time" by sharing their common faith.

A similar committee began in San Francisco, then several others in scattered sections of the country. Finally, in 1937, the need for consolidation manifested itself. Christian Business Men's Committee International came into existence, with Chicago headquarters. The word "committee" puzzled many people, who felt that perhaps "club" or "association" might better describe the organization. However, the word "committee" was deliberately selected. Each man should perform specific duties within a CBMC.

The need for doctrinal unity, since many doctrinal viewpoints came into the picture, resulted in the nine-point Statement of Doctrine that has safeguarded the organization's spiritual status and has helped to maintain a remarkable degree of harmony.

Briefly, the statement sought to encompass the fundamentals of the faith: (1) inspiration of the Scriptures; (2) Trinity; (3) virgin birth; (4) man's sinful nature; (5) death of Christ; (6) His resurrection; (7) His premillennial return; (8) new birth through faith in Christ, and (9) everlasting punishment of the lost.

Only point seven has caused appreciable discussion. Not only amillenarians and postmillenarians, but also some premillenarians, feel that this requisite for committee membership eliminates many men of strong evangelical faith. However, the Board of Directors always returns with the same verdict: since men of God waited on Him for the original Statement of Doctrine it should not be changed. These men seemed to have a sense of urgency about the task of witnessing to their faith, whereas men of other beliefs might be less likely to have the same vision and burden. Finally, the directors say, to change the doctrinal statement at any point would make it liable to change at other points, hence it would gradually become weak. Obviously, some outstanding evangelical men are thus hindered from becoming members of Christian Business Men's Committees.

However, these men are not barred from fellowship and active duty with the committeemen. Rather, they are encouraged to lend their time and talents to the varied ministry of CBMC; and many of them do take part in this way. They may not vote on committee matters, but otherwise they actively participate in the committee program.

As succeeding chapters will show, no two committees are alike. Local circumstances and conditions, among other things, help determine the committee's program. Primarily, however, all these committees aim to reach other business and professional men regarding their commitment to Christ. The statistics available today attest to the success of their endeavor. From the original handful, now some fifteen thousand business and professional men are working together in this unique effort for Christ.

They come mainly from the United States and Canada, but also from thirty-five other countries. No exhaustive statistics have been kept, but fragmentary figures would seem to indicate that this effort has influenced more than five million persons toward a practical faith. Christian businessmen have distributed billions of Gospel leaflets or tracts. They have conducted thousands of open-air, hospital, jail and rescue mission meetings.

Not only little known business and professional men, but also such prominent men as Governor Mark Hatfield of Oregon, Lt. Gen. William K. Harrison of Korean Peace Conference fame, and Alberta's Premier Ernest C. Manning have played varying roles in the organization's history. In CBMC terminology, a business man is anyone who is not a minister, missionary or other full-time Christian worker. All business men are eligible for full membership. The so-called "professionals" in religious work are entitled to associate membership, and thousands have availed themselves of this privilege.

A fifteen-man Board of Directors, with five men being replaced each year, conducts the organization's business. The directors meet twice a year: first at a midyear session in a selected city, then for three days prior to the annual convention, which is usually held in October and which rotates from one area of the continent to another. In the international headquarters office in Chicago, a full-time executive secretary is the board's liaison with the more than five hundred committees. The executive secretary is aided by a director of publications and a staff of five girls doing clerical work and bookkeeping.

Like Gideon's three hundred, the fifteen thousand lay crusaders composing the Christian Business Men's Committee International may seem insignificant in number. Qualitatively, they seek to be "Diligent in business, fervent in spirit, serving the Lord."

CHAPTER THREE

FROM LITTLE ACORNS

"Privately, many feel Christian Business Men's Committee International will one day develop into the gigantic proportions it now only foreshadows. After the war the possibilities of greater interest loom large. Then CBMC will come of age." – Dr. Carl F. H. Henry, now editor of *Christianity Today*, in November 1943

ORGANIZED IN 1930, the Christian Business Men's Committee of Chicago at first stood alone in its active witness. But its increasing fruitfulness eventually sowed the seed for expansion.

In 1936, Dr. Paul W. Rood, president of the Bible Institute of Los Angeles, walked into the office of a San Francisco investment banker. Arnold Grunigen, Jr., general sales manager of J. Barth and Co., listened patiently to his beloved friend.

"Arnold," Dr. Rood began, "back in Chicago is a splendid organization—the Christian Business Men's Committee. It has been organized for more than five years and is doing a wonderful work. But we need one in every city of size in the United States. Could you head the Bay area?"

Grunigen hesitated for a moment. "I'm too busy," he replied. "I'm already teaching the Men's Bible Class every Sunday morning. I . . ."

Dr. Rood smiled pleasantly. "I knew you'd say that. But how else are we going to reach business men? Do they come when you invite them to church?"

"Not too often," Grunigen admitted.

"Christian Business Men's Committee reaches men I can't reach," Dr. Rood continued. "They're invited to lunch and they hear a few testimonies and are offered proof that Christianity does work."

To add weight to his argument, Dr. Rood then recounted the early history of the Chicago committee.

Original members of the committee were A. J. Leaman, C. B. Hedstrom, J. S. Lincoln, Frank W. Sheriff, and Ernest Wadsworth of the Great Commission Prayer League. Sheriff served as first executive secretary of the committee. A Chicago attorney, Paul B. Fischer, drew up bylaws for the local organization and later for the international organization as well.

"If anyone is entitled to credit as 'Father of CBMC,'" attorney Fischer once said, "it is A. J. Leaman. He was the humble pastor of a small Mennonite church on Chicago's west side. To augment his small income, he secured part-time employment with Moody Bible Institute. Burdened for city-wide revival, the last such evangelistic effort having been conducted by Billy Sunday in 1914, Leaman obtained a leave of absence from the Institute."

"In 1914," Fischer continued, "nearly all the churches in Chicago, both orthodox and modernistic, were united in an association of pastors. The association had sponsored the Billy Sunday campaign with considerable success. After 1914, the line of cleavage between sound belief and modernistic unbelief had developed so far that orthodox pastors found it necessary to sever their connection with non-believers. These pastors then formed their own association."

The subsequent confusion within the ranks of the association, leading to suspicion of those outside the association, was leading to the unwillingness of any ministerial group to sponsor a city-wide evangelistic campaign. Meanwhile Pastor Leaman had come in contact with several undenominational groups which he thought had real vision.

"Among these," Fischer said, "were the Gideons, the Gospel Fellowship Club, Business Men's Gospel Teams, Business Men's Prayer Group, Christian Business Women's Council, and Christian Women's Lunch Clubs."

Pastor Leaman called a meeting of the leaders of these groups. He and the leaders planned a six weeks' series of daily noon meetings to be held in a centrally-located Loop theater. To look after these meetings, the Chicago Christian Business Men's Committee of five men was organized. A short time later, members added to the committee included Vaughn Shoemaker, twice Pulitzer prize-winning cartoonist with the *Chicago Daily News,* later with *Chicago's American.*

The first chairman of the committee, Ben Hedstrom, proved to be not only a man of vision but also a spiritual prophet in his own right. Addressing a critic of CBMC one day, he said, "Can't you see that this is the beginning of a movement of God which is to become international in scope? It will be the means of salvation of hundreds, yes of thousands, of men."

Arnold Grunigen listened attentively, with obviously growing interest, as Dr. Paul Rood recalled the early history of the Chicago committee. He responded to Rood's challenge, and San Francisco soon joined the Illinois metropolis with a full-fledged Christian Business Men's Committee. By 1938 five such committees had been formed, and a general conference met in Chicago at the LaSalle Hotel. One hundred and fifty members attended this first of the annual CBMCI conventions. The Silver Anniversary convention met in Miami, Florida, in October of 1962.

At the first international convention in Chicago, delegates elected by acclamation a five-man steering committee: Charles E. Gremmels, industrialist, New York, N. Y.; Grunigen; Hedstrom; Dr. N. A. Jepson, chiropractor, Seattle, Wash., and R. G. LeTourneau, Longview, Texas, industrialist. After the convention these men along with Chicago building contractor Carl Gundersen and others met in a hotel room, prayed for wisdom, and began to form a working organization. Conservative evangelicalism marked the doctrinal statement which they adopted at this meeting. Grunigen wrote a booklet entitled "What We Believe." In it he clearly defined each of the nine points of the

Statement of Doctrine hoping to prevent all misunderstanding.

First international officers included Hedstrom as chairman; LeTourneau, vice-chairman; Grunigen, secretary, and Dr. Jepson, treasurer. Gremmels completed the original Steering Committee. The printed program of the first National CBMC Conference in 1938 gives information about early efforts:

> For seven years God has singularly owned and blessed the work of the Christian Business Men's Committee of Chicago. From Monday to Friday every week, a stimulating and inspiring Gospel service is held each noon hour in the Grand Opera House in the Loop and broadcast over Station WJJD. Thousands of men and women have been won to Christ and thousands of Christians have been helped and quickened in their spiritual lives.
>
> Radiating from this primary effort, the spirit of evangelism has penetrated into the churches by way of special services, conducted and addressed by laymen; successful tent campaigns, and an aggressive program of open-air preaching during the summer months reaching multitudes of those who otherwise might have never heard the Gospel message.

That noonday broadcast has continued down through the years. It is heard from Monday through Friday over Radio Station WMBI, the voice of Moody Bible Institute. In recent years, energetic former bank executive Walter McKeag, chairman of the Chicago committee, presided over the broadcast.

Thousands of letters have attested to the effectiveness of the broadcast. One man wrote: "Eleven months ago, I was sitting in my room on the verge of suicide. I had lost my money in gambling and did not know which way to turn, but I thank God that His Word came over the radio from the noonday service."

Another letter, typical of other letters received in the more than thirty-year ministry of the broadcast, reads in part as follows:

One day after scanning the pages of the early edition of the Chicago Daily News in the vain hope of finding employment, I started east across the Madison Street bridge where I paused for a few moments looking down into the Chicago river. I was thoroughly disgusted with life.

Our home life was a miserable affair and we were on the verge of getting a divorce. As I looked down into the waters, my past and unhappy life came before me and suddenly I had an impulse to end it all by jumping into the river. For some reason unknown to me at the time, 1 was led away from that awful scene to a theater in the Loop where evangelistic services were being sponsored by the Christian Business Men's Committee.

It was there that I heard the truth of God's Word proclaimed, and it was there that I personally received Jesus Christ as my Saviour and committed myself into His hands. I was ordained into the ministry five years ago.

Like many other areas of the CBMC ministry, the air waves have proved highly productive. A fifteen-minute taped broadcast, called Man to Man, contained testimonies of business and professional men in interview form. Many committees sponsored the CBMCI broadcast locally. Radio was only one of the instruments figuring in the steady advance of the movement.

CHAPTER FOUR

THE BABY CONTINUES TO GROW

"In The CBMCI"
by S. F. Logsdon
(Former pastor Moody Memorial Church, Chicago)

Out in the field of service,
　　Scattered to points far and wide,
There by the call of the Master,
　　Standing whatever betide;
Men in their own occupations,
　　Pointing their fellows on high;
God has the choicest of workers
　　In the CBMCI.
Darkness is spreading its shadows,
　　Sin fastens firmer its grip,
Daily the countless of thousands
　　Into eternity slip;
Yet by the wayside the faithful
　　Looking to Him in the sky,
Business men working for Jesus
　　In the CBMCI.
Life with its worldly attraction,
　　Business with money and fame,
Quickly give way to the honor
　　Of serving in Jesus' dear name:
Armed with the sword of the Spirit,
　　Bought with the blood and made nigh,
Men run their business for Jesus
　　In the CBMCI.
Wives of these noble crusaders
　　Joy in their holy design;
Bidding them Godspeed in service,
　　Gladly self-interests resign;
Urging them on in the conquest,
　　Faithful in prayer standing by;
Thanking the Lord for their labors
　　In the CBMCI.

WAR CLOUDS BEGAN TO HOVER over many parts of the world as 1940 arrived. In the spirit of the time, a special committee announced the Emergency Called Conference of Christian Business and Professional Men in October at LaSalle Hotel in Chicago. Fourteen men issued the call: R. G. LeTourneau, C. B. Hedstrom, Boyd Hargraves, of Chattanooga, Tennessee; Andrew Wyzenbeek, Chicago; J. Park McCallie, Chattanooga; B. L. Fisher, Martinsville, Virginia; W. G. Haymaker, Lenoir, N. C. (later to become Billy Graham's Crusade director); Arnold Grunigen, Jr., San Francisco; Dr. N. A. Jepson, Vaughn Shoemaker, C. E. Gremmels, Paul B. Fischer, Clifford Lewis, and Vernon Patterson.

"Since this conference is called for the purpose of humbly waiting upon the Lord and praying for a great spiritual awakening and the evangelism of the world in the shortest possible time," the call read, "the program is planned to give full freedom to the Holy Spirit to move upon the hearts of those present to pray and speak as He may guide."

Two days later, the third annual CBMCI convention met in Chicago. Speakers included a former professional hockey player from Hibbing, Minnesota, Andrew W. Hughes. Twenty-one years later, in 1961, Hughes was elected tenth chairman of CBMCI. His work as comptroller for the Rheem Manufacturing Company in New York City took him into various parts of the country and also into South America. In South America he made many important contacts for CBMCI.

Before 1941 CBMC grew in a variety of ways. Twenty-five local committees became part of the international setup. From its earliest years, the movement had been interested in reaching servicemen with its message of faith. London, Ontario, launched the first CBMC-sponsored servicemen's center. San Francisco, Chicago (in Waukegan first, then also in the Loop), and Detroit followed.

At the same time, several committees, following the example of Chicago, turned to the air waves. Los Angeles, Seattle, San Francisco, Philadelphia, Detroit, and San Diego added broadcasts. Successful telephone ministries cropped up in New York, Washington and Chicago—another activity of the burgeoning lay movement. Though results of the telephone ministry could never be accurately measured, many letters have indicated changed lives as a result of this new approach.

"For five years now," one caller wrote to the CBMC of Chicago, "I've been thinking of accepting Christianity. It wasn't very easy to accept it because I was born a Buddhist and raised as one. At last, I can truthfully say that I have accepted the Lord fully. Thank you again for bringing Christianity into my life. May God bless you and the lady who gave me your phone number."

Classified advertising in the personal column of newspapers usually brought an avalanche of callers. Many callers proved to be earnest seekers, and eventual finders. In 1941 the fourth annual convention met in Philadelphia. At this convention LeTourneau became international chairman; Grunigen, vice-chairman; Jepson, treasurer, and Fischer, secretary. By this time, the nine-man international board also included Hedstrom, Gremmels, Hargraves, R. A. Laidlaw of Auckland, New Zealand, and H. E. Eavey of Xenia, Ohio. Progress seemed slow and deliberate in the early days. In later years the sure and steady foundation paid rich dividends.

CHAPTER FIVE

A VOICE IN THE WILDERNESS

"This is the greatest spiritual movement in the 20th century."
— Dr. Paul Rood, president of the Bible Institute of Los Angeles

THE OLD YEAR—1941—had gone out with guns blazing. Just six days prior to the surrender of U. S. forces on Bataan, the young movement known as CBMCI lost a spiritual giant—Swedish immigrant shoe merchant, C. B. Hedstrom. The passing of this genial Chicagoan proved to be the first breakthrough in the original ranks of CBMC. But this first international chairman left much of the light of his radiant brand of Christianity. His brief message written for the third annual convention reveals something of his spiritual strength and fervor.

"John the Baptist had the answer for those who asked his identity," Hedstrom declared, "He described himself as the voice of one crying in the wilderness. John did not say that he was the great I AM. He made it very plain that he was only the voice of Him who is the Way, the Truth and the Life.

"Many wonder who the Christian Business Men's Committees are; what are their motives; what is their program. Is it a new movement or another denomination?

"We answer thus," Hedstrom continued. "We are only a voice of Him who crieth in the wilderness. Our cry is for God's people to wake up; Christ is coming; get busy for God."

"Our land is full of religious movements that never move anything for God," Hedstrom added. He described CBMC as a forward evangelism program. "It is no selfish movement to start something new or to build a denomination," he said.

"With God's help and through the power of the Holy Spirit we want to be a reviving stimulus to the churches and an encouragement to the preachers who love Christ above anything else and stand solidly on the Book."

Hedstrom then quoted his friend Arnold Grunigen, who had written an explanatory paragraph about the aims and purposes of this thriving lay movement:

"Active, virile laity will combine to preach the blood of Christ, resist all moves to sidetrack us on reformation projects of one type or another, soft-pedal labels, consolidate our lines in order to unify our efforts in getting the Gospel to as many people as possible in the shortest time possible; joining together with the express intent of waging an assault on godlessness, materialism, unbelief and modernism. What the world needs is the Gospel. Do you like our platform?"

Hedstrom's many friends and admirers gathered that he for one did like the platform. His further remarks in his convention address left them without doubt.

"This unique testimony that has been so singularly blessed of God," he continued, "had its beginning here in Chicago ten years ago. It started in prayer. In fact, it was the result of years of fervent intercession by several prayer groups which met weekly in several downtown meetings."

Hedstrom then described how "the Holy Spirit brought them together in an evening of prayer and consultation, out of which was born Chicago's great noon-day Gospel meetings. Originally it was planned to conduct just a month's pre-Easter services, but God gave unmistakable evidence that we should go on.

Here we are after ten years, at an expense of nearly two hundred dollars a day, still going on with the testimony. Now it looks as though we would keep on until Jesus comes."

The shoe merchant vigorously exhorted his hearers to action. "God help us to be faithful!" he exclaimed. "God is in it and to Him belongs all the glory. No man or group of men deserve any honor for this. It simply is God's voice in this present wilderness, this day of chaos, spiritual declension and unscriptural movements."

Hedstrom noted that CBMC in Chicago was not alone in its efforts to stem the tide of wickedness. "Many other similar groups have started in various sections of our land," he said.

"They are patterned after the Chicago committee, but not all are functioning along the same lines. These groups have to meet the requirements of their localities, but all of them have the same objectives. China and other foreign countries are forming similar committees."

Quick to discern possible dangers in any spiritual endeavor, Hedstrom warned the men of the personal sacrifices necessary if success were to crown their efforts. "This God-honored and God-sustained testimony can continue only through men who are unselfishly devoted to the cause of Christ," he said, "men who are wholly surrendered to God and who gladly and willingly obey His command and submit to the blueprint of heaven. Surely if ever God called men to sacrifice to the cause of Christ, it is now.

"Everyone connected with this work," Hedstrom continued, "gladly and willingly gives his time and money that the work of soul-saving might go on. This is the day when God calls men to launch out into the deep in a real effort to 'rescue the perishing, care for the dying, and snatch them in pity from sin and the grave.'"

Ben Hedstrom had a gift of preparing the way for God to bless and a gift of preparing God's people to assimilate His blessing. "What this third international convention has in store for us," he concluded, "we do not know. But God will bring together a band of men whose hearts He has strangely touched, men who have only one desire and that is to be their best for God, men who will listen to the still, small voice and be ready to· go places for Christ."

With the passing of Hedstrom, God raised up other voices from the wilderness. None has proved more faithfully ubiquitous than Texas industrialist Robert Gilmour LeTourneau or more vocally dynamic than Arnold Grunigen, Jr., the California investment banker.

CHAPTER SIX

GOD'S SALESMEN

"We're all salesmen. It's our job to sell the Christian way of life to the top men in business, government and the professions." – Arnold Grunigen, Jr.

THOUGH THE ECONOMIES and sacrifices of war would perhaps limit their efforts, the leaders of Christian Business Men's Committee International, in convention at Toronto in 1943, decided to move forward. They would establish a headquarters office in Chicago with competent secretarial help and a full-time field representative.

Claes V. S. Wyckoff, later to become an advertising executive in San Francisco, became the first editor of *Contact*—official CBMCI publication—from his home in Evanston, Illinois. The magazine began as a tabloid-size paper, emerging into its present pocket-size style in 1945 under the editorship of Clyde Dennis, founder of Good News Publishers, famed for its Tract Club of America and also its Condensed Book Club.

The name of the publication originated from the idea of "contact with God in prayer for wisdom; contact with other Christian men for fellowship; contact with the churches for service; contact with men who need Christ; contact with radio audiences for a wider ministry, and contact with servicemen for witness and fellowship."

In February of 1943, Blair Quick and Charles Cooper became the first two volunteer traveling representatives of CBMCI. They circulated widely among the committees then affiliated with it. What they saw and heard made them more positive than ever that God, in a day when men's hearts were failing them for fear, had indeed raised up a strong band of vigorous witnesses.

In Philadelphia, for example, a man was about to commit suicide. His daughter lay in the hospital with curvature of the spine.

His wife suffered severely with an illness. He feared a foreclosure on his mortgage. One of the CBMC members in Philadelphia invited this man to the weekly luncheon of the CBMC group. The man came, and the testimonies of business and professional men softened his heart. The Word of God, "sharper than any two-edged sword," penetrated his inmost being. He knelt with four men and poured out his heart to God in surrender.

Two weeks later he got a good job; his daughter left the hospital; his wife recovered, and he received a six months' extension on the mortgage. The matter was sealed, he felt, and God had indeed undertaken for him. Apparently the teamwork of Christian business men had again paid everlasting dividends. Their teamwork has been evident throughout the history of the international movement. An incident in the Nation's Capital became one link in the chain of spiritual cooperation. Robert P. Woodburn, vice-president of The National Bank of Washington, D.C., read the newspaper headlines carefully. A prominent manufacturing executive had suddenly disappeared, leaving his wife and family. Four months before he left he had financed a new car through The National Bank.

Woodburn followed the story in the newspapers as the weeks passed. He established indirect contact with the executive by tracing down two bad checks the manufacturer had written against his record. Eventually, the police caught and arrested the executive. Brought to trial, he escaped with light punishment and a rebuke from the judge. Woodburn sought him out for interview.

Confronted by the white-haired banker, the harrowed executive expected a stern inquiry as to his car loan and the subsequent bad checks. That inquiry proved only incidental. Woodburn took time to impress him with the importance of his soul's welfare. The disturbed executive dismissed the subject as over his head. Though Woodburn considered the matter virtually closed, he would continue to pray for the man.

Several months later, Woodburn answered a long distance call from the East. The executive had established himself in a responsible position with a manufacturing concern near New York City. Finding himself despondent, he requested the banker's help. Woodburn again pressed the claims of Christ upon him. In desperation, the executive agreed to make an appointment with a friend of Woodburn's, a Christian business man in the East.

A few days later, Woodburn received a letter from his CBMC friend in the East. He had spent two hours with the manufacturer. The manufacturer had shown faith in God. The former fugitive from justice now seemed to know an inner peace and happiness he had never before known. Again, thought Woodburn, the teamwork of God's salesmen had been used to bring spiritual success.

Another pioneer Christian business man, Frank Burkhardt of Detroit, has told one of the many experiences he had while a witness in CBMC. After speaking at an open-air meeting one day he heard a woman profess her faith. After her profession she asked him to visit her husband and give him the same good news she had heard.

Burkhardt went to their home that same afternoon. At first sullen and resentful, the man soon expressed willingness to listen to the Gospel. Later in the afternoon he professed faith in Christ, responding to Burkhardt's clear-cut invitation. At ten o'clock, while preparing to leave for his work on the night shift, the man had a heart attack and died. That experience, said Burkhardt, served as a continuous reminder of the importance of prompt action on spiritual missions.

Another Christian business man in Detroit one day received a telephone call from a woman. She had fled her apartment because her husband had threatened to kill her. She asked him to go to the apartment and see what he could do. Immediately leaving his office duties, the business man hurried apprehensively to the apartment. The janitor, with whom he talked upon his arrival, confirmed the woman's story.

The business man rang the bell. A scowling man appeared. The CBMC man hesitated for a moment, then said, 'I'm with the _____ Company, but I've come to talk to you about something else. May I come in?"

Sullenly, reluctantly, the man opened the door and let him in. A big knife lay on the table and a fur coat ripped to shreds lay on the floor.

Quietly and simply, yet almost fearfully, the visitor related the miracle of his finding faith in God. The softening and penetrating influence of the Holy Spirit slowly began to take effect. Two hours later, the man dropped to his knees, tears streaming own his face, and he made his peace with God.

Shortly before the business man left the apartment the man's wife returned. Hesitantly, fearfully, she opened the door. Her husband embraced her tenderly. The CBMC minuteman joyfully, tearfully, told her how her husband had found peace. Then he left the apartment.

Experiences such as these gave momentum to the budding lay movement. Business and professional men of many denominations, stirred by the great potential for good the CBMCI showed, began to join the thousands of others who already had taken their places on the firing line for God.

CHAPTER SEVEN

SPIRITUAL WARFARE

The Christian Business Man's Daily Questionnaire.
1. Does my life please God?
2. Do I enjoy being a Christian?
3. Do I cherish in my heart a feeling of dislike or hatred for anyone?
4. Am I studying my Bible daily?
5. How much time do I spend in secret prayer?
6. How long has it been since I led a soul to Christ?
7. How long since I had a direct answer to prayer?
8. Do I estimate the things of time and eternity at their true value?
9. Am I praying and working for anyone's salvation?
10. Is there anything I cannot give up for Christ?
11. How does my life look to those who are not Christians?
12. Where am I making my greatest mistake?
13. Do I place anything before my Christian duties?
14. Am I honest with the Lord's money?
15. Have I neglected any known duty?
16. Is the world better or worse for my living in it?
17. Am I doing anything that I would condemn in others?
18. Do I have a clear conception of my place in the Lord's work?
19. What am I doing to hasten the coming of Christ?
20. Am I doing as Christ would do in my place?

-Selected

IN 1944, WAR RAGED ON MANY FRONTS. By this time, CBMCI affiliations had increased to seventy-five separate committees. The spiritual warfare continued to keep pace with the world conflict. A Salvation Army officer, Major Cecil Zarfas, attended the Toronto convention and later described his experiences there.

"I went curiously to the Royal York Hotel last Saturday night to join some Christian business men who had invited me down to see how Christian business men conduct a meeting. I found myself in a meeting in which my Lord was magnified, in which He had the pre-eminence!

"Let me describe the scene," Zarfas continued. "The huge hall on the second floor of the great Toronto hotel was crowded to capacity, perhaps eight hundred business persons sitting at the tables. Many more unable to gain admission took their places in surrounding galleries. The leader of the meeting said:

"'We are going to sing. You will find songbooks on the tables.' Now, I thought, what kind of songs do Christian business men sing? I was in for a pleasant surprise. I wish you could see that songbook; why, they have revival songs which even the church has forgotten to sing!"

Major Zarfas said Arnold Grunigen had asked the audience to sing "Thank You, Lord, for Saving My Soul."

"My word," the Salvation Army officer exclaimed, "what a chorus and what a sing! And what a witness! Why do I believe we are on the verge of a great awakening? The answer is right here. These laymen, many of whom are engaged in big business, and all of whom are business men from coast to coast in Canada and the United States are placing themselves at the disposal of Almighty God. Here are men who are not afraid to be witnesses unto Him. Here is a Spirit-filled movement that will bring new life and power to the church! Yes, great things are about to break.

"Do you know what these laymen, these business executives, these business men are doing by their witness?" he asked. "They are laying a tender hand on the arm of industry and saying to it, 'In the name of Jesus Christ of Nazareth, rise and walk!' Do you realize what we in the church have been doing for years? God forgive us! We have been seeking to gain the favor of big business. We thought we could get places through resources instead of through faith in a living God! Altars have been broken down; our path has been one of compromise for we could not have the blessing of big business and preach the whole Gospel of Christ!"

Major Zarfas concluded his description with a ringing challenge. "So what is the Christian Business Men's Committee International saying?" he continued. "To every pastor, preacher, and church organization it says: 'On with the Father's business, save souls, bring the people back to the Cross and to Pentecost, seek first His Kingdom, then the light, and the glory, and the power of the Holy Spirit will return!' And as they closed that great gathering with clasped hands, singing, 'Blest be the tie that binds' so I ask you, will you go forth to witness for Him now?"

Major Zarfas called the convention a miracle—the miracle of seeing and hearing men of various denominations, of diverse businesses and professions, unite in proclaiming a common faith in God through Jesus Christ.

Gordon W. Bish, executive director of Canadian Keswick Conference Grounds in Ferndale, Muskoka, Ontario, and an international director of CBMC, reported on a fellowship meeting which had been held in Toronto. More than two hundred men had attended the meeting.

"The Spirit of God was powerfully present," Bish declared. "Men wept unashamed as they resolved by God's help and grace to live victoriously, and live to serve Him. They did more than resolve. Since that time many have testified to the work done in their hearts, and the joy that they now have in witnessing and serving in many places."

The same year Bish gave his report, T. E. McCully, then vice-president and general manager of the Carpenter Baking Company in Milwaukee, later full-time Executive Secretary of CBMCI described his introduction to the international movement. Even before this introduction he was active in Youth for Christ and Gideon work, as well as in the CBMC of Milwaukee.

"In September 1942," he said, "I attended a baker's convention in Chicago and met Bob Swanson. We went up to Paul Fischer's office where we fellowshipped around the Word and in prayer.

Bob and Paul gave me some literature regarding the Detroit convention and asked me to come.

"We in Milwaukee had not realized what we could do," he continued. "We were doing no more than sitting at luncheon meetings, but I came away from Detroit inspired. I determined that by the help of God the CBMC of Milwaukee would seek to do some real work for the Lord."

McCully said that his committee had invited soldiers and sailors to the Monday luncheons. "Some have been definitely led to the Lord," he continued. "This was thrilling and has encouraged us to go on. Early in October we had twelve meetings within eight days, entitled 'Religion in Business.' The Lord blessed us exceedingly. At least seven souls were saved and more than twenty joined the CBMC. One of the biggest things that happened was that the barriers were broken down and we are now working with the pastors of these various churches."

Glowing reports like these encouraged existing and prospective committees. Expansion continued on a steady scale.

Moments of sorrow tempered the joys of spiritual success. Death came to CBMCI Director Boyd W. Hargraves on May 22, 1944, in Chattanooga, Tennessee. His long-time friend Dr. J. P. McCallie described the director's death.

"If that archenemy of mankind, Death, could ever be called beautiful," he said, "Boyd Hargraves died a beautiful Christian death. He was conscious up to the very last and knew that he was going on to be with the Lord. On Sunday morning, at early dawn, he asked his wife, who stayed with him through day and night, 'What day is it?' She replied, 'It's Sunday, a beautiful day.' Boyd said, 'What a grand day it would be to go home.' 'We will take you home,' she replied. 'Oh, no, I mean to my real home; my citizenship is in Heaven.'"

God had other men prepared to "stand in the gap" left by this servant. The spiritual battle continued.

Meanwhile, as the devastating influence of World War II continued to spread around the world, servicemen flocked to CBMC centers, and there sought refuge from the terrors of the war.

After San Francisco had completed its first year of operation at the Center, the CBMC reported more than a thousand professions of faith among the 116,000 servicemen who visited the place. Milwaukee joyfully told of a hundred conversions during the first six weeks of operation at its Center. When Toledo opened its doors for military personnel, Christian business men found two sailors on hand an hour and a half early. God, it seemed, placed his seal on the step of faith at the outset. Both sailors had hungry hearts and made commitments to Christ.

Detroit Christian Service Centers, Inc. saw about two thousand boys make professions of faith in a year at Fort Custer. In addition, the CBMC-sponsored activity there sent four trailer units around from one nearby camp to another, and in little more than a year some 3,600 boys made spiritual decisions. Frank Sheriff reported at least three thousand saved at the Waukegan, Illinois center, and "a great deal more than twice that number in Chicago in a year's time." In ten months, the Center in New York City had forty thousand visitors and three thousand professed converts. A nine-year total showed twenty-six thousand decisions. San Diego told of 3,500 decisions. Minneapolis and its famed Hospitality House reached close to ten thousand boys each month.

Meanwhile on many fronts the battle raged. American forces landed in Guam, U. S. troops invaded the Philippines, and the Germans launched a counteroffensive in Belgium. In this critical year of 1944 the spiritual warfare likewise continued unabated. Christian business and professional men fought and won many battles for the hearts and lives of servicemen, and others.

CHAPTER EIGHT

TWO GIANTS OF THE FAITH

"God has given to CBMC one field in which we are almost alone. That is in
the matter of a positive witness to other business men." - Harry R. Smith,
vice-president and Chicago representative, Bank of America

WITH THE SCENT OF VICTORY permeating the national atmosphere
in 1945, Christian business and professional men continued to take
advantage of many opportunities—both ordinary and unique—
to tell others of the faith that was keeping them steady in the
midst of chaos and confusion.

By V-J Day, more than a hundred committees had swelled the
ranks of CBMCI. At the eighth annual convention in New York
City, R. G. LeTourneau still ruled as international chairman,
with Arnold Grunigen as vice-chairman and Paul B. Fischer as
secretary and treasurer. By now the board had been increased to
fifteen members. Blair Quick remained as field secretary.

Through the early years, one of the movement's most active
witnesses had been Charles E. Gremmels, one of the five founders
of the international, president and director of the Providential
Realty and Investing Co., Inc., New York City. In 1945 Gremmels described several opportunities typical of those which had
come his way.

"While in the Midwest, attending a convention," he said, "I
spoke at several outside meetings that had no connection with my
business or with the convention. A fine-looking man remained
after one service and showed deep concern. He was the heir of a
celebrated chemical family."

Gremmels added that this man "had come seeking help to set
his house in order." The New York executive had referred to a
text in II Kings 20:1, "Set thine house in order." His listener had
responded to the challenge, and the joyous appearance he showed

at subsequent meetings convinced Gremmels he had indeed set
his house in order.

The same week, while en route to Texas, the investment
executive offered a New Testament to a serviceman riding with
him. "The serviceman responded by saying he had a ministerial
brother-in-law whose consistent faith he respected," Gremmels
said, "but he admitted that he himself was enjoying no similar
experiences. I witnessed to him of my having found the joy of
the Lord.

"A few weeks later," Gremmels continued, "the pastor brother-
in-law wrote me expressing his thanks and that of his wife (the
serviceman's sister). The train incident had so greatly impressed
the young soldier, he had written them that he was reading the
New Testament daily and wished we had met earlier."

The same week Gremmels had still another opportunity.
"Three soldier lads crowded with me in a front double seat in a
day coach from Jacksonville to Miami," he said. "The boys said
they were returning to a camp at Fort Lauderdale from a Pacific
campaign. All three had been shipwrecked and related incidents
in the shipwreck coupled with, 'We sure were lucky.'"

Gremmels then referred them to the guiding hand of their
Heavenly Protector. "This they then acknowledged," he said.
"At my request they prayed with me, their heads bowed in the
crowded train. Then for more than two hours, off and on, they
read some thirty tracts I had given them. They passed the tracts
on to their buddies with approving comments."

"They gave me their addresses," Gremmels continued, "and
I later sent them each a New Testament. They had lost theirs
in the shipwreck. They asked if they might keep the tracts for
further use, and I added other tracts to help them. The dining
car waiter asked for additional gospels of John for the kitchen
crew. So before I had reached Miami, several hundred tracts and
thirty Gospels and Testaments had been distributed by hand—
on that first leg of the trip alone. My supply was replenished sev-

eral times in the next ten days of personal work in Miami, West Palm Beach, St. Petersburg, Nashville, and en route home."

Gremmels often reminded CBMC associates and others that "there are golden opportunities of personal evangelism on trains, buses, taxis, and at stations, hotels, and dining places. Also on business errands we must gladly act on the Master's Word: 'They need not depart, give ye them to eat.'"

Never one to use old age as an excuse, Gremmels continued his fast pace of witnessing well into his eighties. He often related an experience he had in 1945 at the Marine Hospital on Staten Island.

On his normal assignment to visit the patients, sing for them, distribute tracts and write letters for some of them, he came across a man on the critical list. A man came from behind a screen and walked away from the patient. Gremmels heard an intern say, "Well, it serves him right. He isn't fit to live or to die."

Anxious to help if possible, Gremmels approached the intern. "Is the patient able to be visited?" he asked.

"Well," the intern replied, "you won't want to talk much with him. He was brought in here last night, cooked alive from a tug steam pipe which bursted. I shot enough dope in him to kill a dozen men and still he groans and screams. He sure is a tough one. Nothing we can do will ease the pain. I don't know why he's living. We sent for a minister of his faith, but he only cursed and drove him off."

Gremmels thought for a moment. "May I go speak with him?"

"If you don't mind the same thing happening to you," the intern replied, an amused smile on his face.

Approaching the bed, Gremmels saw a man almost fully wrapped in bandages. Only two fingers and the corner of his mouth were uncovered. Bending low, Charles Gremmels began to speak softly. "My friend," he said, "I'm sorry to see you suffering. I wonder if you would like me to pray for you."

Out of the corner of his mouth, the patient whispered. "Bend down low, buddy, and let me smell your breath."

Gremmels complied with the strange request. "Okay," the man said softly, "make it snappy, fellow. I drove the other man away because his breath was like that of the oiler who neglected to watch the gauge. It's because of this oiler that I'm cooked alive and am suffering in torment and hell. Do something for me, will you?"

Gremmels bent down low. "You mustn't strain yourself," he said quietly. "I'm going to pray, and if this is the prayer of your heart, pinch my hand to indicate agreement. God, be merciful to me, a sinner, and save me, for Jesus' sake." The two free fingers tightened their grasp. The patient gargled and was gone. The intern stared at the man. "Look at that face," he said to Gremmels. "Why, he's still smiling like a baby."

Other Christian business men also tell of deathbed conversions they witnessed. Another of the five original CBMCI founders, Dr. N. A. Jepson, the Seattle chiropractor, tells of radio broadcasting.

"The Christian Business Men's Committee in Seattle has been broadcasting daily except Sunday for nine years," he wrote in 1945. "At present we are on four stations: KEVR, Seattle, the originating station; KTBI, Tacoma; KRKO, Everett; and KVOS, Bellingham."

Dr. Jepson then added that "God has given us the very finest talent, both instrumental and vocal, spiritual and willing. Evangelists, Bible teachers, missionaries, pastors, and others of God's choicest saints have helped, so that we feel the program has the blessing of the Lord every day. Twenty minutes is employed in the musical part of the program and announcements, with ten minutes for the message.

"Frequently we are able to turn over the facilities to a local pastor and his evangelist during special conferences or evangelistic meetings," Jepson continued. "This we are glad to do, putting on the musical part ourselves and having the evangelist give the message."

The chiropractor added that "listeners send in special requests for the unsaved and the sick. As announcements are made concerning these requests, some listeners jot down the names of those persons about whom they feel especially concerned. Our listeners' many answers to prayer, for salvation and for health, have been a real source of satisfaction to our committee.

"A large proportion of our speakers," Jepson said, "are missionaries from fields all over the world. We keep in touch with these speakers, and read reports of their work over the air to keep the radio audiences interested in these missionaries. We are more than ever convinced of God's blessing, whether in the church or on the radio, when the missionary vision is followed. This way we keep good contact with our Christian audience."

The Seattle pioneer declared that "at the beginning of our work, we asked the Lord to so work that when a family became interested, He would bring salvation to the whole household. That prayer has been abundantly answered in many cases. Prayer certainly helps in getting contact with radio audiences. Psalm 62:5, 'My soul, wait thou only upon God; for my expectation is from Him,' is potent."

It was not only in radio broadcasting that the year 1945 saw giant strides made toward a more effective witness on the part of business and professional men. New ideas, new enthusiasm, new methods—all combined to increase the outreach of this lay evangelistic arm of the church.

CHAPTER NINE

PLAIN VANILLA

"CBMC is a graduate school of Christianity, a hardy place of service for wholehearted men." - Arnold Grunigen, Jr.

THE FIRST FULL YEAR OF PEACE—1946—brought a strange paradox: everything but peace on the home front. Labor fought capital as never before, with four and a half million men involved in strikes. Congress and President Truman fought over price controls. The Big Four victors wrangled interminably over peace treaties.

The nation was preoccupied with peace—the U.S. nonfiction best-seller was Peace of Mind. But business and professional men found little evidence of peace in the hearts of most men, whether they were in labor or in management.

Tragedy came to the Arnold Grunigen home, as official word finally confirmed the "killed in action" verdict on Corporal David W. Grunigen. He had been shot down in a B-29 just after completing an incendiary bombing mission to Kobe, Japan, on June 5, 1945. Thousands of the friends of the CBMC dynamo assured the bereaved parents of their prayerful sympathy. The God of all comfort, the parents said, gave peace of heart and mind. In spite of the tragedy, the full program of CBMC continued on all fronts.

Also in 1946, evangelism played a major role in the outreach of the eight-year old movement. Dr. Hyman J. Appelman, Jewish evangelist, reaped a spiritual harvest of 829 professions of faith and 329 rededications in a campaign co-sponsored by the CBMC of Orlando, Florida and the local Baptist Minister's Association. That was only one of many efforts Appelman conducted with CBMC approval. The evangelist has been a staunch friend of the movement down through the years. Similarly, such evangelists as Billy Graham, Torrey Johnson, Merv Rosell, Jack Wyrtzen,

Charles E. Fuller, and many others, have worked closely with the laymen.

Back in the early thirties, about twenty-five members of the Christian Business Men Committee of Charlotte, North Carolina, felt an unusual burden of prayer. Gathering on the Frank Graham farm before daylight one morning, they went to a pine grove in back of the house. Fasting all day, they spent the hours from sunrise to sunset on their knees in the pine needles.

"What we prayed for," one of the committeemen said, "was that the Lord might raise up a man who would take the Gospel to all the world and turn men in far places to Christ. Here we were praying for such a man and all the time he was right there on the place." But twelve-year-old Billy Graham, lanky and athletic, had little idea then of the mission that awaited him in years to come. "I wonder what those fanatics are doing here," he said to others of the family.

Because twenty-five business and professional men took time out of busy lives to pray, God heard and answered. More than fifteen thousand believers today—men of many denominations— have seen prayer result in God's miracle-working power. These stalwarts of the faith include farmers and clerks, doctors and lawyers, butchers and bakers, governors and mayors. They have one thing in common: a consuming passion for the salvation of others and a desire to share their faith with other men, especially with those who are not likely to hear the Gospel in any other way.

In other earlier years, it was mostly Hyman Appelman who teamed up with CBMC in citywide campaigns. In a two-week campaign in Portland, Oregon, he had the full support of CBMC. Nine hundred commitments resulted. A CBMC member, Leonard Fleischmann, served as vice-chairman for the evangelistic effort. Nor was that the last of intensive campaigns in 1946.

The city of Buffalo, New York, found itself stirred during a three-week Appelman campaign. Of 2500 persons who made decisions, more than a third professed conversion. Local CBMC member Elmer D. Weigert served as chairman for the campaign. Other Christian business men assisted him.

The varied program undertaken by CBMC offered work for every member. In most committees, each member could find an avenue of service to appeal to his taste. Even with the nation no longer at war, the service centers continued to reach thousands of soldiers and sailors. The CBMC of San Diego, reporting on the center there, listed a total of 8,556 professions of faith within one year. For years the San Diego Center has been maintaining its heavy schedule of entertaining servicemen.

In this same eventful year of 1946, Claes Wyckoff elicited from a reluctant Arnold Grunigen some of the common sense thinking that accounted for and explained his upswing as a successful business man.

"I believe enthusiasm is a vital essential to any business man," Grunigen said. "Application comes next. During my road experience I made it a definite practice to finish Wednesday's reports on Wednesday night. Before retiring I always made a complete program for the next day. And I studied my job; I made a business of it."

Grunigen continued, "I realized that if I lacked in years I need not lack in knowledge. Perhaps the most outstanding qualification that any man can possess is the ability to build confidence. I have always tried to make such a pleasing impression that my next call would be still more welcome. Lastly, I believe in my job and the firm I represent. As long as I'm here, I'm going to give them the best that I have."

A history of CBMCI would hardly be complete without at least one typical Grunigen message, though printed words cannot hope to show the verbal dynamite and obvious sincerity in his spoken word. In 1953 the Californian spoke at the annual banquet of the CBMC of Tucson, Arizona. His theme was, "Christianity Works Today."

"Gentlemen," he began, "it's a great joy to be with the Christian Business Men's Committee of Tucson at this their annual banquet."

Grunigen then explained his presence in the city, "I am here at the Arizona Inn for a meeting of the National Association of Security Dealers. Twenty-one of us from all over the United States meet for the next three days and I'm glad to have this interlude before we go to work because we'll be sitting in meetings all day every day for three days. I'm here tonight to talk to you about the most important thing in the world: the most important thing *your* life."

Grunigen lost no time in reaching his main point. "Life can be a very superficial, unsatisfactory thing; or it can be a full-orbed, wonderful thing. Christianity makes the difference. Not religion, but Christianity."

"I choose to distinguish between Christianity and religion, he continued. "Christianity is not exciting or meaningful to lots of Americans, but it ought to be. Our Christian beliefs are suspected of being trite and flat and unreal. But that is definitely not true. Constant, exciting discoveries are to be made in the Christian life if we will only try it."

The San Francisco extrovert rarely called attention to himself deliberately, but he had just gone through an experience completely new to him. "I want you to forgive me," he said. "I'm going to do something that maybe I shouldn't do, and I don't want you to think I'm an exhibitionist. I don't want to work on your feelings, because I'm a cold-blooded stock broker. I operate on people's pocketbooks. It's the only way I've ever earned my living: by selling investment securities to discriminating investors. When I tell you the little story that I'm going to tell you now, it isn't to work on your feelings but to illustrate in a practical way what I mean when I say that Christianity works today."

The audience sat expectantly, almost eagerly. Grunigen's manner and words lacked nothing of the old fire. "Very unexpectedly, on the night of December 21, in my home in Atherton, California, I fell out of bed. Mrs. Grunigen had to call a doctor. They carried me off to Stanford Hospital in San Francisco. When I came to, and they had let me rest for a day or two, a brain surgeon told me that in order to find out what the trouble was they were going to have to put two little holes in the back of my head, take the water out, and put air in; then take X-rays."

The investment banker was not one to hide the truth. "Now I'm a sissy," he said. "I'd never been sick. I'd never been in a hospital. But I didn't like what the doctor told me. He's a Christian, so I said to him, 'I don't like any part of what you're talking about, but can we have a word of prayer together?' You see, that's the way I feel about Christianity. I think it's that practical. He said, 'Sure we can.'

"Afterward he said, 'I'm coming in after dinner to cut your hair off.' That didn't sound good," Grunigen admitted.

"After dinner he came in and said, 'I have to take half of it off, or do you want it all off?'

"I said, 'No, let's just take half.'

"When the family said good night, and I was there all alone on that night of December 27, 1954, for the first time in my life I was completely at the end of myself.

"For the first time in my life," Grunigen continued, "my confidence and assurance were gone—just what I needed all my life as salesman and sales manager was gone.

"I said to the Lord, 'You know what a sissy I am. I've never had anything happen to me. You know what a scaredy-cat I am. I'm going to be a wreck for that doctor in the morning. I'd like to sleep, if You'd let me.' And I turned over. And believe it or not when I reached for my watch the next time, it was four o'clock in the morning. And for me that was a miracle. It wouldn't have been for a lot of people, but for me it was.

"I believe in this Christianity stuff so much," he continued, "that I said, 'Thank You, Lord.' The Christianity I'm talking to you about is just exactly that practical. When you're at the end of yourself, God loves to do things for you. The man who comes to the end of himself and doesn't have Christianity—faith and trust in Jesus Christ—in his heart, that man has no place to go. I don't want to trade places with any man or woman in that spot.

"When I began in the business world," Grunigen continued, "I was told to keep my mouth shut about two things: religion and politics. Since I have been in business, we have shot the works on politics. There's only one place where we still keep our mouths shut, and it's completely wrong. That's on our religion: Christianity."

His arms waving emphatic gestures, the Californian seemed determined to leave no oratorical stone unturned. "Until we begin to gossip the Gospel, until we begin to tell each other what makes us tick, we haven't lived up to our opportunities in America. One of the signs indicating that we haven't grasped the real benefits of living in a free country like America is the fact that we are still ashamed and unwilling to talk to each other about the great, eternal verities of the Word of God.

"And so help me," Grunigen added, "until America gets to the place where business men from coast to coast are willing, in Rotary, Kiwanis, Lions, Elks, Moose and Eagles, to let people know that we go to church, that we sing hymns, that we read the Bible, that we call on God, that we depend on Him, that we're not trying to be Christians, we're *trusting* to be Christians— unless we get to that place America will not continue to get the blessing of Almighty God.

"It's perfectly ridiculous," he continued, "for preachers, priests, and rabbis to be carrying the whole load. They can't do it. Until butchers, bakers, and candlestick makers, stenographers, nurses and all, join the group of extroverts who are willing to spread the good news that Christ died to save sinners and that old-fashioned Christianity is available, until we all do that, the news isn't going to get out.

"Until men are born of God," he said, steering clear of theological terms, "government and society and philosophy and science will be evil and get worse. Man does what he does because of what he is, and you cannot ignore the Word of God and expect prosperity indefinitely. In fact, your boys and girls and mine are probably going to have to face a terrific situation and we had better lead them to God through Christ so that they can face the problems of life."

An illustration came to Grunigen's mind as he prepared to end his message. "I want to read to you," he said, "about one man who made just one mistake." Then he read from a clipping: "He brushed his teeth twice a day with a nationally known and advertised toothpaste; his doctor examined him twice a year; he wore his rubbers when it rained; he slept with the windows open; he stuck to a diet with plenty of fresh vegetables; he relinquished his tonsils and he turned in several worn-out glands; he golfed but never more than eighteen holes a day; he got at least eight hours sleep every night; he never smoked, drank, or lost his temper; he was all set to live to be 100; *but the funeral will be held Wednesday.*"

"He is survived by eighteen specialists, four health institutes, six gymnasiums, and numerous health foods and antiseptics. He forgot God. He lived as if this world was all. And he is now with those who say: 'The harvest is past, the summer is ended, and we are not saved.' Guess his name: The Typical American."

"Plain vanilla" was one of Grunigen's favorite terms. Working to shun frills of any kind, he hoped to keep utter simplicity his standing rule, even in public speaking.

"Often," Grunigen said in obedience to his rule, "when I talk to the Rotary, Kiwanis, or Lions, I say, 'Fellows, there's going be a last Rotary meeting; a last Kiwanis meeting; a last Lions meeting. But there *never, never, never* will be a last meeting for Christians for God's Word says, 'the world passeth away, and the

lust thereof: but he that doeth the will of God abideth forever'
(I John 2:17).

"I hope that those of you who have never had an encounter
with God will say before you walk out tonight, 'God forgive me!
I've never told You that I'm a sinner; I've never thanked You for
sending Your Son Jesus Christ to die on the cross for me. You're
speaking to me, Lord. I want to do what You want me to do. I
put my faith, hope and trust in You. Please help me from now
on; I want to be a Christian.'"

Grunigen ended his speech with thoughts based on Romans
6:23. "Through simple faith in Jesus Christ you can begin to live
forever, *today*. 'For the wages of sin is death; but the gift of God is
eternal life through Jesus Christ our Lord.'"

The Grunigen messages, of which this message is typical,
sowed many seeds of faith that later came to fruition.

CHAPTER TEN

'LET GOD DO IT'

Profit and Loss

I counted dollars while God counted crosses;
I counted gains while He counted losses!
I counted worth by the things gained in store,
But He sized me up by the scars that I bore.
I coveted honors and sought for degrees;
He wept as He counted the hours on my knees.
I never knew till one day by a grave
How vain are the things that we spend life to save.
I did not yet know till a friend went above
That richest is he who is rich in God's love!

-Selected

BY 1947, SOME 162 CHRISTIAN BUSINESS MEN's Committees had been formed, largely in the United States and Canada. Coming of age in several respects, the movement added its first fulltime executive secretary. Donald MacDonald, a former Fruehauf Trailer Company executive in Detroit, came to the Chicago office from his position as executive secretary of CBMC in Detroit.

During his nine years at the international headquarters, Mac-Donald saw many changes. He initiated improvements such as the two-color lapel pins and the official charters issued by the Chicago office to affiliated committees.

MacDonald made a survey of the work of the committees. Forty committees sent him reports showing 7,952 open-air, hospital, jail and rescue mission services conducted by CBMC men in 1947; 625,000 tracts distributed, and 30,541 professions of faith. Only one-fourth of the committees had sent reports. MacDonald thought that simple arithmetic would reveal staggering figures on an international scale.

MacDonald's two four-page Gospel leaflets, "I Lost my Religion" and "A Church Member, But Lost," were top sellers for years. His work on *CBMC Contact* magazine involved hours of night work in addition to his regular time in the office.

In the July-August 1947 issue of *CBMC Contact*, a steel fabricating executive, Edward B. Stirm, of San Jose, California, expressed the sentiments which he saw as common to many Christian leaders.

"It is often true," Stirm wrote, "that when a Christian man first hears of the work of CBMC or comes into contact with a live and active committee for the first time, his eyes are opened to 'what God can do' with a group of men who are willing to 'let God do' instead of 'doing themselves.'

"Often the man had never known before," Stirm continued, "that the impossible can still be accomplished by God through the ordinary business man. He had seen the organized church fail in reaching men with the Gospel, and yet here were ordinary business men demonstrating a method of reaching other business men with the Gospel in an effective way. Never before had he seen a group of Christian men from many denominations and church backgrounds working together without quibbling about nonessentials, because they kept their eyes on *Christ*.

"And so his enthusiasm has been kindled, his activity increases, his burden for the lost business men of his acquaintance becomes great and he pitches into the work of the local committee.

"But before long a still different development shows itself. This new member awakens to the tragic condition in his own church, and he gets busy there. The pastor recognizes the zeal of his newly-awakened Christian and puts him to work. Soon he is so engrossed in the work of his own church that the 'outside' work of the local committee gets only the 'tag ends' of his time.

"God's program, however," Stirm continued, "is going forward even though it appears that the very work that was instrumental in sparking workers to get busy for the Lord seems to get the short end of the deal. But if God can, through CBMC, restore to useful service a Christian man who had lost interest in the Lord's work, then should committee members all shout, 'Praise the Lord!'"

Stirm concluded by pointing out that "God's ways are past finding out. Who are we to question His methods of accomplishing His purposes in the world? Whether the service being rendered for the Lord is through the agency of the committee or through an organized church, it is the Lord who blesses and He who gives the increase. God has used CBMC as His instrumentality in the past, and He will continue to use it in the future, so long as we 'let God do' instead of 'doing ourselves.'"

Stirm's thinking had its effect on CBMCI members. As the delegates assembled together in convention at Kansas City, Missouri, they seemed newly cognizant of a Spirit-led future. A London insurance broker, William J. R. Horsburgh, attended his first such convention. He became the first Honorary British Representative for CBMCI, and for a number of years gave it valuable service in the British Isles. Out in the "grass roots" of the organization, the program of the movement seemed to be getting Divine approval.

Down in Tampa, Florida, a dramatic struggle took place in the heart and life of the tennis champion of that city.

"On April 10, 1947," declared the athlete, "I was in fine physical condition, in excellent spirits and financially secure. I wouldn't have traded places with anyone I knew. The next morning at daybreak I lay flat on my back, totally paralyzed afraid that I might die any minute and just as fearful that if I lived I would be a helpless cripple."

The Tampan had always been athletically inclined, his main interest being tennis. In his college days at Florida Southern, he was captain and number one player on the varsity team. After college he kept up his tennis and in 1946 became the city singles champion of Tampa at the age of thirty-six. Defense of that title led to his downfall.

"In playing a fellow about half my age," he said, "I overex-
erted myself in a futile attempt to overcome his youth with my
determination. After two hours of running in the hot sun, I lost.
After taking a shower, I started home. But on the way, I stopped
at a tavern and drank a glass of beer. Immediately afterwards, I
felt as if I would pass out. Finally, however, I managed to make
it home. Soon afterwards my reflexes began to leave me. After a
night of torture, I awoke to find myself in that paralyzed condition."

Since an earlier experience had strongly influenced the tennis
ace against God, he gave no serious thought to calling on Him
for help. "In the crash of 1929," he said, "my father lost everything that he had, and when this happened I never prayed to God
again. In 1936 my mother died suddenly and I blamed God for
this also. I had been brought up by fine Christian parents and
had attended Sunday School and church regularly for many years.
My folks had taken me to all of the evangelistic meetings that
came to town, including those of Billy Sunday.

"In 1936," he continued, "I married and my life was nothing
but business and pleasure. I played tennis at every free moment,
which included all day on Sunday in spite of my wife's objec-
tions. She wanted me to go to church with her, and I did so
on rare occasions, just to please her. She tried to warn me what
would happen if I continued pushing myself so hard. In spite of
her warning, I would play tennis almost to the limit of my endur-
ance, then sit up late playing poker and drinking."

By 1945, the tennis enthusiast had gone to church with his
wife often enough to gain election as an officer. "I knew nothing
about God's Word," he said, "and cared less. We had selected
this church because of its fine social atmosphere. I became good
friends with the pastor and looked up to him as a fine Christian
leader. I was puzzled, though, by his answers to my questions.
I found his spiritual interests were confined to the here and now.
He wasn't concerned with, nor did he ever mention, the here-

after. This mystified me, because my strict religious upbringing had left me with the idea that a Christian's purpose in life was to get ready for the day when he would go to be with God."

The Tampa star then told of his eventful year of 1954. "An acquaintance of mine," he said, "had been inviting me each week to a luncheon of the Christian Business Men's Committee. I had turned down his invitation several times, since I didn't want to be seen in the company of a group of religious fanatics. One Friday morning when this man came in, however, I had no excuse and he knew it. I agreed to go."

The Tampa committee at this time was in its infancy, and only four men attended this luncheon. "Directly across the table from me," the athlete said, "was a man whom I had known only as a kind of underworld character. His presence at a meeting like this was a mystery to me. His calm smile and sparkling eyes intrigued me. I had always imagined him to have a calculating look in his eyes and no semblance of humor.

"After the meeting," the tennis star continued, "I couldn't resist asking him what had happened to bring about the change in him. He told me how his wife had prayed for him for eighteen years. Her prayers had been answered the year before and his life had changed completely. Even though I could see and sense a terrific change in him, I couldn't understand what had brought it about."

As he left the meeting, the athlete was handed a little booklet. It was called "What We Believe" and contained a detailed description of the nine-point CBMC Statement of Doctrine. "I stuffed it into my pocket," he said, "and promptly forgot about it. In fact, I could hardly wait to get to a stag party at the golf club for a session of poker and free liquor."

"The following afternoon," he continued, "after arriving home from work, I sat in my living room talking with my wife. I happened to pull the little booklet out of my pocket and began to leaf through it idly. I saw some startling statements. No doubt

I had heard them many times before, but this was the first time I had ever associated them with my own personal needs.

"The booklet said that God's only begotten Son, Jesus Christ, had died on the cross for the sins of the world, including mine," he said, "that if I would repent, ask God's forgiveness for my sins, and take Jesus Christ as my own personal Saviour, He would immediately give me eternal life. I read this to my wife. As the urgent necessity for someone greater than myself to take over my problems became clear, I determined to take these statements at face value. I was not sure they were true, but if they were, I wanted to give God the opportunity to take over my problems for me.

"With my wife as witness," the Floridian said, "I asked God to forgive my sins, and I received Christ as my personal Saviour. I told Him I would try, with His help, to do His will at all times, whatever the cost, even if it meant losing my friends and being considered a fanatic. When this decision failed to make me feel differently right away, doubts began to arise in my mind. I asked my wife what she thought I should do next. Even though she was not yet a Christian, I believe God gave her the answer. She suggested I should pray and ask God for guidance and help.

"That evening, before going to bed," he continued, "I said what I believe was my first prayer in twenty-five years. Then I dropped off to sleep."

Next morning, the athlete found himself doubting God again. He got out of bed and walked toward the kitchen, wondering just where he stood with God. "Suddenly," he said, "to my utter amazement, it seemed God spoke to me in a clear, unmistakable way. 'Don't worry another minute,' He seemed to say. 'I heard you, I believe you, and I accept you. Now go and do My will.' This shocked me so deeply that for many seconds I stood transfixed. As soon as I was able, I called for my wife - so loudly that she ran to me thinking I must have fallen and hurt myself.

"Though she was skeptical at first," he continued, "in a few minutes she began to realize that a supernatural thing had happened and was still happening. She felt the presence of God for the first time in her life. 'The whole day is just like it must be in heaven,' she said. 'The grass is greener, the flowers prettier, and the sun brighter than I ever knew before.' God in His infinite mercy knew how much I needed that assurance. Never since have I doubted my salvation."

The Tampa champion went on to tell of the complete change in his life. "The things I once loved, I now hated," he said. "The things I once hated, I now loved. Even the desire for the things of the world dropped from me that very day. Uppermost in my mind was a desire and determination to love God above all else and to tell others about the wonderful life He had given me and wanted to give them.

"God used my salvation," he concluded, "to help save members of my immediate family. Since then my wife, my brother and his wife, my sister and her husband have all been saved. My life now centers around the things and people of God. My church and CBMC are the focal points for men and women to find God and spiritual fellowship."

Though mass figures sound impressive, it is the individual that must be reached before he becomes part of a total number. The Tampa tennis star is one of the individuals whose lives have been affected for eternity through the ministry of CBMC. As new committees were added to CBMC in the forties, the enthusiasm among local members and leaders alike grew daily.

CHAPTER ELEVEN

MILITARY ALLIANCE

Why thou couldst ever love me so,
And be the God Thou art,
Is darkness to my intellect,
But sunshine to my heart.

-Selected

"A YEAR OF JITTERS" best described 1948. Russia gobbled up Czechoslovakia, and Whittaker Chambers opened up a pumpkin containing State Department secrets. Harry Truman upset the prognosticators, defeating Thomas E. Dewey in the presidential election. Dale Carnegie and Alfred Kinsey wrote best-sellers.

In this jittery year, Colonel Cecil R. Hill of Indianapolis, Indiana, met Robert P. Woodburn, banker in Washington, D.C. Woodburn introduced him to CBMC. "My fondness for Christian Business Men's Committee was almost a case of love at first sight," Col. Hill said. "I had never seen a group of men so devoted to the Lord. The annual convention of CBMC came to Washington in October of 1948, and what I saw and experienced there thrilled me beyond measure. I had never seen anything like the way those men gave themselves to the Lord.

"I became a regular worker at the CBMC Victory Center for Service Men in Washington," Col. Hill continued, "and began to see the Armed Forces as a great mission field. More and more, the Lord laid it on my heart to form a fellowship of born again servicemen as a witnessing group in the Armed Forces."

In early 1951, Col. Hill was transferred to Camp Atterbury, Indiana. There he found a group of enlisted men holding regular Bible study classes and prayer meetings. The Army officer began to attend the Indianapolis CBMC meetings regularly. At one of these meetings, a member of the CBMC asked him what the committee could do to encourage the evangelistic work at Camp

Atterbury. At a subsequent banquet, with servicemen as guests, a resolution was adopted which brought into existence the Christian Military Men's Committee. The CBMC of Indianapolis became the father and sponsor of CMMC.

"Hundreds of servicemen," Col. Hill said, "have found their way to the Lord through the witness of CMMC. Its members are urged to join CBMC after they leave the service. We urge them to join it even before they are discharged, if location permits.

"In Korea," he explained, "CBMC and CMMC work as a team. The chairman of the first CMMC in the Korean Armed Forces at Kyung-ju was Lt. Col. Lee Kyung Wha. After he was discharged from the Army, he organized a CBMC at Kampori. Being a physician, he provided free medical service for Koreans using his work as an opportunity to witness to them about Christ."

Tragedy came to Dr. Lee in 1956 when his hospital in Kampori was burned to the ground. "But this great soldier of the cross," Col. Hill said, "merely started over again from the bottom and is continuing his effective ministry.

"That same spirit of indomitable faith in Christ, evident in hundreds and even thousands of Koreans, will assure victory to Korea," continued Col. Hill, "a spiritual victory that will not be dimmed by such secular matters as war and its attendant chaos and confusion."

Col. Hill was transferred from his Korean duty to Fort Campbell, Kentucky, as Comptroller. Before his retirement, he organized both a CBMC and a CMMC in Clarksville, Tennessee, which was adjacent to the Army post. CBMCI directors appointed him as CBMC Military Representative. Though CBMC and CMMC have worked closely together in some areas, no practical way has yet been developed or discovered for a cooperative ministry on a widespread scale.

The great potential remains. Many servicemen will eventually become business and professional men. It is CMMC's responsibility to seek to lead the servicemen to Christianity. It is CBMC's privilege and obligation to nurture them in the faith and challenge them to more zealous and effective sharing of their faith with others.

CHAPTER TWELVE

REVIVAL IN NEW ENGLAND

"Help me, oh Lord, to remember that three feet make one yard, sixteen ounces one pound, four quarts one gallon, and sixty minutes one hour. Help me to do business on the square. Make me sympathetic with the fellow who falls by the wayside in the struggle. Keep me from taking an unfair advantage or selling my self-respect for a profit. Blind my eyes to the petty faults of others, but reveal to me my own." – A Business Man's Prayer

THE NATION WAS STILL JITTERY when President Truman made his 1949 announcement: "We have evidence that within recent weeks an atomic explosion occurred in the U.S.S.R." Chiang Kai-shek retired from the presidency of China, and near the end of the year came the Chinese Communist capture of Chung-king.

In Christian Business Men's Committee, it was the year of the big change. The new international policy rotated board members. The directors replaced five of their fifteen-man number each year. No director could serve for more than three consecutive years. Both "Mr. Big's" of CBMCI—R. G. LeTourneau and Arnold Grunigen—came up for replacement.

New York City baking executive Robert S. Swanson became third chairman of CBMCI. He brought a sterling Christian character and outstanding organizational ability to the task. As LeTourneau later pointed out, God's provision of leadership proved His hand upon the movement. Some 197 committees now comprised the international.

During these changes, the articulate Mr. Grunigen, still sounding a clarion call for consistent witnessing, did not hesitate to speak.

"CBMC is one of the significant movements of our day," he declared. "Its membership should include only men who know the discipline of the grace of God, who will not rest on past religious experience, and who despise the average type of professing Christianity which is distinguished by appalling shallowness.

"We invite men of personal courage, who are not easily disheartened, who do not slide back and forth, who are not fickle to join us. If you are willing, God helping you, to operate within Spirit-directed plans and are not overly impressed with any thoughts of grandeur or dramatic flare, for this is truly a warfare, we need you. This operation drafts you into its holy service."

His crusading attitude doubtless attracted hundreds of men into the movement. Also helpful in attracting members was the statement of CBMCI policy which appeared in the March-April 1950 Issue of *CBMC Contact*. The statement clarified the purpose of the organization for members and non-members alike.

"The CBMCI," the statement read, "is an association of Christian Business Men's Committees of evangelical faith whose purpose and aim is to make Christ known as Saviour and Lord. The only reason for our existence is our objective and that is to reach men for Christ through ways and means that are not ordinary.

"We seek to accomplish our aims and purposes through the following activities and methods:
1. Man-to-man aggressive evangelism.
2. Testifying by our life and conduct that Christianity works.
3. Demonstrating that Christianity works in business.
4. Conducting fellowship activities for the purpose of reaching other men for Christ, such as breakfasts, luncheons and banquets.
5. Burnishing and inspiring fellow Christians into a closer fellowship and devotion to Christ.
6. Evangelizing as God gives opportunity through open-air and jail meetings, service men's centers, county farms, rescue missions, etc.

"While we are cognizant of the role we play in God's over-all economy or program, our prayer is that He will keep us (as well as others) from overestimating our importance. We realize also the necessity of being true to the aims and purposes of our organization. For this reason we reiterate the position of the international and affiliated committees.

"We are not: (1) primarily a sponsoring organization; (2) primarily financial underwriters; (3) booking centers for sundry enterprises; (4) an endorsing agency; (5) anti-crusaders. We believe that the only effective approach to better government and improved world conditions is through and by the proclamation of the Gospel."

Also in 1950, revival showers brought refreshing rain and blessing to several of the 212 committees in operation. In Boston, for example, Secretary Fred T. Corum reported that "a flame of revival fire has struck Boston. It began with the prayers of God's people. A committee made up mostly of members of the Boston CBMC under the leadership of Dr. Harold J. Ockenga, pastor of Park Street Church, sponsored the bringing of Dr. Billy Graham as evangelist.

"Our committee chairman," Corum continued, "was Allen C. Emery, Jr. Emery is a CBMC director, a Boston wool merchant, and a son of the chairman of the committee which brought Billy Sunday and also Gypsy Smith to Boston a generation ago."

Corum added that "the committee planned a watch-meeting at Mechanics Hall and then a ten-day service in a local church. But the meetings continued for eighteen days. The largest buildings couldn't hold the crowds. When we couldn't get Mechanics Hall, we rented the Opera House and finally the Boston Garden. At no meeting could all the crowds get into the buildings.

"At the final service, January 16, about sixteen thousand jammed the Boston Garden and about ten thousand more couldn't get in. It was the largest crowd ever to come to the Boston Garden, even larger than when Winston Churchill spoke there or when former President Roosevelt was there.

"A simple Gospel message under the anointing of the Holy Spirit was given by Dr. Billy Graham, president of Northwestern Schools Minneapolis, Minnesota. He is the son of a North Carolina dairy farmer, a graduate of Wheaton College, and a leader in the Youth for Christ movement. He came to Boston fresh from a city-wide revival in Los Angeles, where thousands accepted Christ as their Saviour. Even several Hollywood stars discovered that the greatest pleasure in life is in serving God."

Corum concluded his report with the enthusiastic declaration that "Boston - New England - America is ripe for revival. We need a great ingathering of souls that are precious in the sight of God. A great mid-century revival is on. It should sweep the continent. All over New England the churches are interceding for revival. The largest auditoriums in the larger cities will be used to continue the revival. In April, it will be continued again in the Boston Garden."

With the added blessing of revival came increased responsibility. CBMCI Vice-Chairman Harry R. Smith, vice-president of the Bank of America, San Francisco, sounded the warning.

"Now," he said, "suddenly every city wants an evangelistic campaign. Surely every member of the CBMC rejoices in the fact that men and women are being awakened to their need of the Saviour. But let us not forget that the work of the Holy Spirit can be hindered by men whose lives are not what they should be.

"In our laudable desire for evangelism," Smith continued, "let us not forget that we need first a thorough heart searching. Let us as Christian men fall on our knees and ask God to search us and to cleanse us thoroughly, and to humble us, and to energize us by His Holy Spirit. Lord, send a revival and let it begin in me."

Executive secretary Donald MacDonald then had the assistance of two young women in the international office on LaSalle Street in Chicago. The movement's expansion had necessitated the extra help. Arnold Grunigen sat in the Chairman's position - as he did in 1950, 1951 and 1952. At the thirteenth annual convention in Ottawa, the dynamic keynoter again sounded his crusading note.

"We were too cozy and comfortable before CBMC," he said. "We have now been catapulted into an operation that calls for some sacrifice specializing in the cross. We were luxuriating in rich fellowship with congenial men. Operation CBMC calls for and demands action, doing something about what we believe. That is simply not comfortable, nor is it natural. The natural state of a Christian reminds me of a sign found in a forest in the state of Maine. It reads, 'Attention, Hunters! Don't shoot anything that's still! It may be my hired man!'"

CHAPTER THIRTEEN

HIS HAND AT WORK

"Subconscious prayer of a twentieth century Christian while consciously
voicing more orthodox petitions."

By Richard Woike
President, Richard Woike Co., Inc.

O thou pleasant, comfortable, kindly, good-natured God,
How glad I am that I can look forward
With a reasonable degree of certainty
To another ordinary day.

Keep me today from anything that may tax my faith.
From discomfort, from unnecessary strain, from unusual problems,
Especially those involving sickness or death,
Or the necessary of extending financial aid to relatives or friends,
Dear Lord, deliver me.

Grant that nothing may occur which will disturb
My satisfaction with the way I am, the things I say,
The thoughts I think, the acts I do,
Or the many deeds I leave undone.

Give me this day, in addition to my daily bread,
The butter, meats, and sweetmeats
That are my necessary diet.
And let me not be troubled by qualms of conscience
Concerning the amount of time and money
I spend on food and clothing; pastimes good and bad,
And those pursuits which, while not of spiritual value,
Are the accepted hallmark of the normal citizen
Of this enlightened community in this enlightened age.
Should strong temptation come my way,
Help me above all else to be a gentleman
Who will not embarrass by word or deed
Those who are my companions at the moment of temptation.
Forgive me, in advance, if I embarrass Thee
By failing to identify myself as one
Who seeks to honor Thee in my ways.

Let my conformity to this world's ways
Be limited, O God, to things which,
While some may question them,
Will not, I pray, be positively sin.

About the future
And the darkening trend of things,
Keep me from thoughtfulness.
Events rush on: the world travails:
Can screaming headlines prove Thy Hand's at work
This very moment, bringing near
That fateful cry, "Behold, He comes"?

O, Lord, such disconcerting thoughts!
Keep me from worrying about such things,
And guide me safely to and from
My office, and my home, Amen.

AGAINST A SPECTER OF NATIONAL and international tension in 1951, the Christian Business Men's Committee movement seemed to retain the blessing of God on its effects. A prominent Baptist editor described the movement of that time.

"One of the outstanding developments of this generations," wrote John W. Bradbury in the September 27, 1951, issue of *The Watchman-Examiner*, "is the independent laymen's movement known as the Christian Business Men's Committee. While most of the members belong to churches, their activities are of an independent nature and depend upon a camaraderie developed in the Christian spirit.

"Devoting themselves largely to evangelism," Bradbury continued, "these businessmen are frequently very active soul-winners. In some places, they assume responsibility for the development of community-wide evangelistic meetings which result in the salvation of many souls. They represent a cross section of evangelical Christianity and reveal full sympathy for every evangelical pastor."

The editor added that "in many centers, CBMC represents the most active section of the laity. While boasting that they are undenominational, the members nevertheless belong to and frequently are active in denominational churches. It is good to see these brethren at work. Their efforts to propagate the Gospel in every way available to them are most encouraging.

"They set a good example to other laymen to be active soul-winners," Bradbury concluded. "Their influence reaches beyond the borders of this country to other lands showing laymen how they may engage in work for Christ."

CBMCI leaders appreciated Bradbury's words. They nevertheless pointed out that the movement made no claims of undenominationalism—rather it felt that it had an interdenominational nature.

Meanwhile, in 1951, stories of conversion continued to encourage the leaders and other members. No one activity, it seemed, could claim superiority in sowing seeds for spiritual fruitage. The Lord was using the activities in a variety of ways and with individuals in scattered parts of the world.

A currency exchange official in the Midwest related one of his 1951 experiences. "On February 27, 1951," he said, "I was locking the door of the exchange when two men came out of nowhere, one holding a gun to my side and the other a gun to my neck, keeping me in front of them. They forced me to unlock the door and took me through the double steel door, then ordered me to open the safe.

"I knew I couldn't open the time lock, but how could I convince these holdup men? They struck me on the head with the butt end of the gun and told me they would burn my fingers and feet if I didn't hurry and open the safe. They also threatened to kill me if I refused any longer.

"They hit me again and told me this was my last chance. Right then I knew I would have to convince them it was a time lock. That very moment when I was bewildered and nervous and shocked, God graciously whispered, 'Why don't you tell them to place their ears above the combination and listen to the tick of the time lock?'"

The exchange official followed the suggestion. "They pushed me to the floor," he said, "and ordered me to keep my face down.

One stood guard over me while the other listened. Then he said, 'It's a timer all right. Let's get out of here.'

"While I was lying on the floor wondering what was going to happen to me, the other fellow said, 'What are you going to do with him?' The first fellow had started to go. He called back, 'Just hit him on the head, and he'll lie there a long time.'

"I prayed that he wouldn't hit me again, and God answered my prayer. The fellow standing over me left with the other one.

"For the next few days I was in a state of nervous shock. Then Monday, March 5, 1951, I was listening to the noonday service of the Christian Business Men's Committee. Dr. William Ward Ayer was preaching about Paul and Silas in prison. 'Where are *you* hiding?' Dr. Ayer asked. The enclosure of the currency exchange, with its bulletproof glass, had made me feel that I too was in prison. I looked into the radio and said, 'Lord, I've been hiding in that currency exchange for more than ten years.'

"On that memorable day," he said, "I was breaking under strong conviction. The soloist sang, 'God Leads Us Along,' with its chorus, 'Some through the waters, some through the flood, some through the fire, but all through the blood.' I said, 'Lord, I've never been through the blood.'

"I realized," the official said, "that I had been holding on to the world with one hand and trying to hold on to the Lord with the other. I said aloud, 'Lord, You saved my life, now what do You want me to do?' I also realized that had I been killed that night, my soul would have been in hell. Next day in the currency exchange, I gave up the struggle, surrendering my heart and my life to the Lord."

Again, a CBMC activity had been used to change the life of an individual. In a different area of the country and in a different activity, a second change took place in the life of a man.

"In my youth some thirty years ago," declared Joseph G. Sills, a Hungarian Jew and a building contractor in Washington, D.C., "I stopped going to church because to my mind the church was too dogmatic, too strict, and in many ways too antiquated.

"For all these years," Sills continued, "I didn't go near a church. Although I tried to live a clean and honest life, I slowly forgot even how to pray. About two months ago, on the invitation of Robert Woodburn, I went to the luncheon of the Christian Business Men's Committee. There I saw a group of men, all reflecting happiness and contentment because—as I found out —they had accepted the Lord Jesus Christ as their Saviour."

Sills admitted that for a few weeks he had felt as an outsider among these men. "It was because I still wandered in the darkness," he said. "Five weeks ago, after a lot of meditation, I finally saw the light. Kneeling down in my first prayer of repentance, I too accepted the Lord Jesus Christ as my Saviour. I dedicated my life and my soul to Him.

"I'm a different kind of man now," Sills concluded. "I'm a saved soul. I'm filled with overwhelming gratitude to God for my salvation, and I thank all those who helped me find this wonderful Saviour. May the Lord bless them, and may He use me as one of His faithful sons."

Transformed lives are the dividends which CBMC men eagerly anticipate. They feel they are rewarded frequently enough to keep their spiritual batteries charged and their spirits high. One such dividend they received in Whittier, California. So unusual did it seem to the *Weekly Pictorial* that the publication gave it feature coverage.

"Although it is doubtful," the editors wrote, "if anyone ever declared that religion and real estate would not mix, it is decidedly out of the ordinary when a real estate broker makes a point of combining the two in himself and apparently with great success."

The story went on to say that "the broker in question is Ray W. Davenport, a tall, enthusiastic ex-Texan who, according to local real estate annals, has sold more real estate over the past half dozen years than any other individual. His religious fervor has kept pace with his salesmanship to such a degree that he has attracted a good deal of attention even in Whittier, a city where strong religious convictions are hardly exceptional. Nor are they uncommon, it should be added, among real estate people here.

"Ray's youth," the editors continued, "was spent on farms in Vernon, Muleshoe, and Enochs, Texas. The latter, according to the 1930 census, had a population of 10. He rode twenty-eight miles on a school bus to Littlefield High School, where he was a three-year basketball letterman and salutatorian of his class. Meanwhile, he recalls, 'I helped out on the farm. I picked cotton until I was twenty. We had ten cows and I milked them, and I was twenty years old before I saw my first street-car or two-story building. My career in selling began when I was ten.

"'Lloyd, my brother, and I used to sell watermelons and cabbage but we had to protect our crops first. We used to sleep on a cot in the middle of a field a mile and half from home with a shotgun in case the jackrabbits started after our melons. Our hobby was carving our initials on turtles; one of them walked forty-five miles from the place we first caught him."

The *Weekly Pictorial* editor then took up the story. "Like many young people reared on a farm," he wrote, "Ray had an urge to travel. One of the skills he had taught himself was the art of miniature engraving—'the smallest writing without a magnifying glass'—and he proceeded to groom himself for a traffic inspection job by traveling around the country. He paid his way by engraving watches, rings, and other jewelry, often at fairs and expositions. He also went from college to college where, for a quarter, he would write a fraternity brother's name and address on his watch - 'it took me only a minute.'

"He explains his current preoccupation with religion," the *Pictorial* continued, "by the fact that 'for nine years after we were married, we hardly ever went to church. Then we came to Whittier and attended the Methodist church regularly.' But the first of two turning points in his spiritual life came when he was invited to attend the Saturday morning breakfasts of the Christian Business Men's Committee."

The editor then described the nature of these breakfast meetings. "They consisted of devotions, hymns, and religious testimony," he wrote, "participated in by thirty men representing fifteen different denominations. Davenport began attending in May, 1950, and as a result visited a different church every Sunday.

"Then," the editor continued, "last September 14, he heard evangelist Billy Graham preach to a hundred thousand in the Rose Bowl. 'I surrendered,' Ray Davenport says in relating this experience. 'I walked down the aisle and rededicated my life to the service of Christ.'"

The picture feature concluded with a report that "Ray carries his religious devotion into the activities that make up his daily routine. He generally carries a Bible on his person. His billfold is crammed with religious tracts including the creed of the CBMC, whose motto, 'Broadcasting the Gospel,' he wears on a lapel pin. At the beginning of the interviews on which this article is based, he startled the writer by bowing his head for prayer that it would serve a useful Christian purpose."

In addition to ordinary CBMC functions such as the breakfasts which Ray Davenport attended, an occasional extraordinary ministry finds its way into a local program. One such ministry began in Kansas City, Missouri, in 1951.

With a quartet and three or four business and/or professional men, the CBMC met with eight different trade unions and found a good response at each. Chairman Carl Bechtel has spearheaded this effort for more than ten years. In addition, the CBMC sponsors a fruitful work at the Heart of America Servicemen's Center.

The passing of giants of the faith made more imperative than ever the infiltration of existing committees by younger men. Out in Seattle, death came to Dr. N. A. Jepson on February 19, 1951, his sixty-third birthday. Loved ones and fellow committee members paid glowing tribute to him. Some fifteen hundred people from all walks of life paid him their last respects. But even as grieving pallbearers laid him to rest, the glowing reports from the movement's largest committee would have brought him great joy.

The committee in Detroit, Michigan—long one of the largest groups in the movement—issued a six months' report which cheered local and international leaders. In fifteen city hospitals, members had been responsible for 1,350 commitments to Christ; in three city missions, 95 commitments; in two hundred boys and girls Bible clubs, 3,950 commitments. That brought the monthly average to 889 commitments.

Extending these figures to take into account the 239 Christian Business Men's Committees in operation, members, and leaders felt they had good reason to look ahead optimistically.

CHAPTER FOURTEEN

'CHICKEN AND EGG' MAN

"Surely we have a right to expect a real movement of the Holy Spirit among us, because the God of Jacob is the same today as then. 'Happy is he that hath the God of Jacob for his help, whose hope is in the Lord his God'" (Psalm 146:5).

–Waldo Yeager, president, Cortland Produce Company, Toledo, Ohio

IN 1952 THE CHRISTIAN BUSINESS MEN'S COMMITTEE of Washington, D. C., brought in Billy Graham as its first hotel luncheon speaker. It was an undisguised effort to confront top business, professional and political leaders with the matter of their eternal welfare. Five men responded to Graham's invitation, making commitments of faith.

In Cadillac, Michigan, a nine-year-old lad and a seventy four-year-old grandfather figured in an evangelistic campaign. At a CBMC-sponsored Victory Crusade, with Dr. Harry McCormick Lintz as evangelist, young Gary Gray of Lake City, Michigan, responded to the invitation one night. He remembered hearing his mother and father pray earnestly for his grandfather, John Hausam, of Cadillac. Gary decided to invite him to the Crusade.

The next night, the crippled grandfather accompanied the lad to the evangelistic meeting. A clear-cut message and gospel appeal brought immediate response. The elderly gentleman hobbled down the aisle, his grandson by his side. On subsequent nights, the two "babes" in Christ—sixty-five years apart in age— came to the Crusade together. "A little child shall lead them. . ."

Elder citizens in the CBMC movement heard an encouraging word from the international chairman. "Retired executives will find a thrilling place of service in CBMC," Arnold Grunigen declared. "Many are eager, willing and able to serve, and here is a real outlet. These men are invaluable to our operation. In the 65-69 and 70-74 age groups we have men who can perform yeoman effort by visiting local committees."

Many senior members rallied to the call. Their ability to work with younger men has solidified the organization's efforts in its twenty-five-year-plus history.

Strangely, perhaps, CBMC's blessings have fallen numerous times on the female contingent as well as the male. A retired missionary, Miss Mildred Mosier, of Demarest, New Jersey, attended the 1952 convention in Atlantic City. She had twenty-one years of service in Burma.

"I was greatly blessed," she wrote, "by attending the convention. All of the sessions were good. What a unique fellowship across denominational lines, true unity of the Spirit, a minimum of organizational wheels, and all born-again laymen (and their wives) looking for Christ's premillennial return."

At this same convention, Toledo's "chicken and egg" man —Waldo Yeager, president of the Cortland Produce Company— provided the first change in international leadership in three years. The fifteen-man Board of Directors elected him as chairman. Yeager's sincerity and deep spiritual insight have made him a favorite among audiences in all parts of the United States and Canada. On his later trips abroad, crowds in many foreign cities acclaimed his message.

The Toledo Blade carried a story in 1952 about Yeager and his firm: "Each Monday from 12:30 to 1 p.m. production is at a standstill at Cortland Produce Co., 4107 Lagrange St.

"Lunch time? No, church time.

"For ten years nonsectarian noontime religious meetings have been held for employees of the poultry and egg concern, Waldo Yeager, manager, said. He stressed that all employees are paid for the meeting time—which is in addition to their lunch period— whether they choose to attend or not.

"The majority of the firm's forty workers do attend, Mr. Yeager said, adding that they represent many different creeds.

Folding chairs are set up for the service, held within a short distance of the chicken processing line."

Yeager's tract, entitled "Life's Most Amazing Fact," published by the American Tract Society, has been a top seller.

"A prominent business and civic leader," Yeager wrote in the leaflet, "once invited me to take five minutes to tell his club what I felt was the most important fact in the Bible.

"'I'll be glad to,' I told him, 'and just to be sure you still want to go through with the deal after knowing what I would tell them I'd like to tell you right now just what I believe to be the most important as well as the most amazing fact in the Bible.'

"The civic leader smiled. 'It's a deal,' he said.

"'Okay,' I began. 'By way of introduction, let me remind you that perhaps you think I'm a pretty good sort of a fellow, an average businessman, at least; a good husband and father. But you don't really know me.'

"'My wife and my two boys,' I continued, 'know me a little better than you do, and they are quite charitable with me and consider me a decent kind of husband and dad. But you know, even they don't really know me.

"'There's only one Person who really does know me,' I said, 'and that's God Himself. He knows all about me, my weaknesses, the myriads of things that I would not dare to expose, even to my own family. Yes, He knows *all* about me, and here's the amazing fact—*He still loves me!*

"'Can you imagine that?' I asked. 'The Lord knows all about me, from the inside out, and He still loves me! Don't you agree that this is an important as well as an amazing fact?'

"My friend's face suddenly was serious. 'I certainly do,' he said, 'and I wish you'd tell the club exactly what you've just told me.'

"It was my happy privilege," Yeager continued, "to repeat the story to that group of businessmen, and to see a heart hunger that caused them to invite me back again. For, when all is said and done, nothing in life really matters except that God loved me enough to do something about it, by sending his only Son to die on the cross that I—and you—might have everlasting life, simply by trusting in Him and accepting Him into our hearts and lives. Then it becomes our privilege to live for Him and witness to His saving grace and keeping power.

"'If thou shalt confess with thy mouth the Lord Jesus (Jesus as Lord), and shalt believe in thine heart that God hath raised him from the dead, thou shalt be saved' (Romans 10:9).

"Won't you take advantage of life's most amazing fact by recognizing and believing that God knows all about you, and *He loves you just the same!*"

That selected sermon, along with scores of other sermons written by CBMC men, has led to numerous inquiries and commitments in all parts of the world. Publicity regarding the movement continued to increase as the results mushroomed.

More and more, it seemed that impartial and unprejudiced voices outside the organization trumpeted the merits of this powerful lay witness. A world at war—even though the hot phase raged only in Korea, while armistice negotiations continued—paid little heed to the voice of religion as far as a national response was concerned. Increasingly, however, individuals in all walks of life bent listening ears to the message of faith, the message widely heralded by business and professional men of various denominations.

CHAPTER FIFTEEN

GOD'S PLUMB LINE

"The secret of CBMC continuing on for God to become an even greater power and influence is dependent on each individual member keeping the supply lines open. There is absolutely no substitute for a day-by-day, prayerful meditation on the Word of God." – T. E. McCully, vice-president and general manager, Carpenter Baking Company, Milwaukee, Wisconsin

WITH THE DEATH OF JOSEPH STALIN on March 5, 1953, Malenkov became Premier of the Soviet. Dag Hammarskjold assumed duties as United Nations Secretary General. In this country, Dwight D. Eisenhower's inauguration as President claimed the spotlight early in the year. The Christian Business Men's Committee in Washington, D.C., alertly took advantage of the inaugural occasion.

An Inaugural Souvenir, prepared for CBMC, contained photographs of Eisenhower and Nixon, a brief biography of each man, and a map showing the route of the inaugural parade. Inside the folder, a section entitled "Living Americans Speak" carried significant spiritual messages in brief from such men as Lt. Gen. William K. Harrison and former Olympic track star Gil Dodds. Members of CBMC distributed one hundred fifty thousand souvenir folders.

Equally alert to open doors, members of the CBMC of Orlando, Florida, headed by insurance executive Don Mott, traveled to the northern part of Florida on an assignment.

"The young insurance executive," *Moody Monthly* recounted, "stood with head bowed, waiting expectantly. He had poured his heart out - a simple lay testimony, but saturated with the Word. Now he watched for God to work.

"His youthful audience, some eighty first-time offenders who had come voluntarily to the afternoon service, sat in thoughtful silence. Evidence of conviction shone on many faces, but no one stirred."

The writer added that "a plain-spoken, simple invitation, impressing Romans 10:9-10 on the hearts of his hearers, had no immediate effect. The soft strains of a hymn seemed to charge the atmosphere, but still the boys sat in silence, though lines of conviction seemed to etch themselves on several faces.

"The speaker reminded his listeners that they could not leave the hall without making a decision. It was heaven or hell, happiness or sorrow, success or failure. The quiet singing continued. Still no one stirred."

Don Mott bowed his head and prayed again. He was confident that God would answer the prayers of his CBMC quartet members and himself. While traveling the more than four hundred miles from Orlando to the Apalachee Correctional Institution in northwest Florida, they had asked for twenty-five commitments.

"Now they waited," the writer continued, "the quartet members, J. D. Peck, Ossie Clerico, Tom Vickers, and Robert Johnson, assured in their hearts that God would give the increase. They prayed as never before.

"Breaking the awful silence that had followed the invitation, one of the boys—unashamed of his tears—made his way slowly to the front of the hall. He gripped Mott's hand, confessed Jesus Christ as Lord and Saviour of his life and stood facing the other boys.

"Mott, youthful but zealous chairman of the Christian Business Men's Committee of Orlando, repeated his simple invitation. Another boy went forward. Then another. The Holy Spirit's presence became like a convicting pall over unbelievers and like a sweet savor to those who named the name of Christ."

Tear-stained faces became more evident as first one, then another of the boys went forward. Now they went in pairs, then more than two at a time. Finally, all but fifteen or twenty of the boys stood at the front of the hall. Mott and the quartet members counseled with them, rejoicing in the Lord's goodness.

"Within a few days," the article continued, "several of the youthful converts asked Paul J. Eubanks, superintendent of the institution, if they might start a Bible class. Meanwhile, the other boys had followed the example of their buddies, and had accepted Christ too.

"Said Superintendent Eubanks: 'We were thrilled at the response and interest indicated. This interest is continuing to grow.' Again, the effective testimony of laymen—whose hearts and lives the Lord has touched—had borne fruit to His glory."

Conscious of a continuing need for dedicated men, a need proven by the Florida assignment, CBMC leaders repeated frequent reminders along this line. T. E. McCully, then vice-chairman, summed up his views on the type of men God wanted in CBMC.

"It was in March 1951," he wrote in *CBMC Contact*, "that we were gathered together with 2500 men from all over the United States and Canada at the American Society of Bakery Engineers Convention at the Edgewater Beach Hotel in Chicago. We heard the executive vice-president of the U.S. Chamber of Commerce, over whose desk goes practically everything that transpires in our nation.

"He said to those 2500 men, 'I want to say something to you this morning that I can't say to every audience. America is well on its way to slavery. Only one half of one percent of the people of the world have been free people since Christ was born. America has been the freest of the free. Why? All we have to do is stop and think and go back to our forefathers and see how they founded this country.'"

McCully then quoted the speaker as saying, 'I'm not a preacher nor the son of one, but I want to say to you men that unless America returns to God we'll all soon be slaves."

"Truly," McCully added, "we are living in the midst of a grim century. You and I were once slaves of sin and Satan, but by the marvelous, matchless grace of God we have been set free. 'If the Son therefore shall make you free, ye shall be free indeed: Thank God for this glorious liberty into which we have been brought and this wonderful fellowship of the CBMC. It's like the old Scotch lady said, 'It's better felt than telt.'"

McCully continued by asking these questions: "What kind of a CBMCer are you? What kind of a committee would your CBMC be if everybody in it were just like you?

"Here is a measuring stick," McCully continued. "Am I separated? Am I a preference man? Am I strong? Am I fit? Am I expert? Am I fearless? Am I active? Am I a numbered man? Am I a man of exploits?"

Then the Wisconsin executive illustrated a spiritual truth with an illustration from the sports world. "I'm a pretty poor golfer," he said. "When I hit the ball, sometimes it will go a little way down the fairway. Then after three or four putts I'll finally get it into the cup. But suppose one day by a mighty marvelous miracle, Sammy Snead comes to live in me. I step up and swing, and that ball goes down the fairway almost to the green on the first shot.

"One approach shot and I'm on the green," he continued. One putt and I'm in the cup. Instead of having three or four over on every hole, I'm getting birdies. As the people watch me, they say, 'How in the world can he do it?' I can't do it. It's Sammy Snead in me."

McCully then reminded his readers that "you and I can't live the Christian life. We'll fail every time. It's Christ living in us that enables us to do it. May God help us to know something about being strong for Him!"

In this same year of 1953, City Judge James Welch of Lakeland, Florida, attended a public auction on the courthouse steps in Bartow.

"Judge," an acquaintance asked him, "do you know Jesus Christ as your personal Saviour?" The question jolted Jim Welch. He mumbled a reply before beating a hasty retreat. Subsequent days brought hours of reflection on his past.

His life had been one of plateaus. He had been ever reaching, ever grasping—in an effort to climb the next rung to personal happiness and success. But with each new level attained, the ladder seemed to collapse and he would start anew.

Jim Welch first sought athletic achievement. After playing high school football, he had received a football scholarship to Pacific University in Forest Grove, Oregon. He would become a star, a gridiron hero, and all the girls would love him. A leg injury quickly ended this dream.

Unable to participate in sports, he wrote for the college paper, covering the activities of athletic performers. He hoped his writing would give him satisfaction and prestige. After three years of school, he joined the Grant's Pass (Oregon) *Daily Courier* as a sports writer. That bubble burst in March 1942 when Jim joined the Naval Air Corps.

Welch attained his commission and Navy wings, but with that proud day of accomplishment came a gnawing realization of a need for something else. After further training at Fort Lauderdale, Jim became a torpedo bomber pilot. But even that and his subsequent marriage to Evora Lewis did not completely fill the void.

On a secret mission—flying radio-controlled aircraft—Welch went into the South Pacific. Action came fast and furious as he flew radio-controlled drones with television cameras and transmitting equipment mounted in the nose. But even that excitement failed to fill his void.

After the war, he finished law school at the University of Florida in 1948. He began his own law practice and became active in civic affairs. In 1951, James Welch won honors as Young Man of the Year in Lakeland, Florida. A year later came his appointment as city judge, youngest man in the nation to hold this position. These accomplishments had still not brought him to the pinnacle of success and personal satisfaction. Honesty compelled him to admit he was not really happy.

A realtor in Lakeland, Ken Harris, invited Jim Welch to the weekly luncheons of the Christian Business Men's Committee, held in the New Florida Hotel. Welch went along for two reasons. He couldn't think of a good excuse for not going. Since Harris brought him considerable business, he didn't want to offend him.

During subsequent weeks, the city judge heard a number of business and professional men tell about their faith. They seemed to have that for which he had been vainly searching. One afternoon, following the weekly CBMC luncheon, Welch was miserable as he returned to his office.

"Usually," he said, "my phone rings about every two minutes. But that afternoon as I sat there, nobody called. It was quiet. I tried to work but couldn't. I just sat and sat and worried. Finally, right there, I just said, 'Lord, I've got to have some help. I'm a lost sinner. Show me what to do.'

"I felt a real release," Welch concluded. "I turned my life over to the Lord there in my office. A tremendous burden was lifted from me. I didn't understand, and still don't, the miracle of it. But I know from that day forward, things have been different. That elusive plateau had been reached."

Today James Welch is highly-respected in Lakeland, Florida. He had found a purpose in life, a reason for living. A Christian business man, "diligent in business, fervent in spirit, serving the Lord" had faithfully discharged his duty to his fellow man.

Meanwhile, the spread of CBMC continued as new committees sprang up in Pusan, Korea; Cork, Ireland, and Mexico City, Mexico. T. E. McCully became international chairman for 1953-54 at the sixteenth annual convention in Chicago. In a major address at this convention, Vice-Chairman Harry R. Smith asked the delegates, "How's your performance?"

The Bank of America executive began with a brief outline of his message. "As business men," he said, "we certainly are expected to be practical. After we have established our purpose, after we have turned on the power, after we have surveyed our privileges, the thing which counts finally is performance.

"We have fed upon His Word," Smith continued. "We have discussed methods, practices and policies. The question now is, 'What are we going to do about it?' James tells us to be 'doers of the word, and not hearers only, deceiving your own selves. For if any be a hearer of the word and not a doer, he is like unto a man beholding his natural face in a glass: For he beholdeth himself, and goeth his way, and straightway forgetteth what manner of man he was.'"

Two questions and subsequent replies composed the next portion of Smith's address. "What is performance on the part of a persuader?" he asked. "Is it something that we do? Yes, it is certainly something that we do. But I believe that it is first, and more important, something that we are. As the saying goes, 'What you are speaks so loudly that I cannot hear what you say.' In our homes, on our committees, in our offices or factories, or wherever we work, what we are will be very persuasive, more so than anything we can say. The quality of our performance will depend largely upon the kind of life that we live in front of our families, our neighbors and our business associates.

"God also commands us," Smith continued, "that we should love one another. Someone once prayed, 'God, make me good, and when I'm good, make me fit to live with.' So many people, who are trying to be holy, are the most uncomfortable people to be near because of the 'holier-than-thou' attitude. You just don't want to be with them. As my own pastor once said, 'To live above with saints we love, oh, that will be glory! But to live below with saints we know; well, that's a different story.'"

Harry Smith then painted an imaginary picture for his audience. "Suppose, for a moment," he said, "that the Lord Jesus Christ were to appear here in person today, and would say, I have decided to come back to earth, but I need a body in order that I might do the work that I have in mind to do. Is there a man here who will, so to speak, step aside and let Me have his body so that I might walk where I want to walk, speak what I want to speak, and do with my hands what I want to do?'

"'You mean to say that You want me to step aside, and let You come in; and that instead of going where I want to go, You're going to walk off with this body?'

"'Yes, that's what I mean.'"

Concluding his message, Smith exclaimed: "What a privilege that would be! Yet that's exactly what God wants to do with your body and with mine, in the person of His Holy Spirit. He said, 'I want to come in. I want to take control. I want you to set your will aside, and let Me do My will. I want you to set your plans aside, and let Me follow My plans.'"

In his own CBMC activities through the years, Banker Harry R. Smith gave evidence that he practiced what he preached. His walk measured up to his talks at numerous CBMC conferences and retreats.

Leaders of a weekend CBMC conference at Cannon Beach, Oregon, rejoiced at a letter received from a man who had attended.

"I feel," the man wrote, "I just can't put off writing you my thoughts of Cannon Beach. I don't believe there was a more needy soul on the grounds than myself. I have been almost dazed of late over church and home troubles. I was conscious of God's helping hand most of the time, but the waters were so disturbing.

"Cannon Beach," he continued, "calmed them through Jesus Christ. Now there is a calmness, a sureness of footing that was never there before. Scales dropped from my eyes, and I was permitted to see a sample of heaven there. Such harmony among all, a spirit of genuine humility, love for the brethren, giving in to the other fellow. It's most amazing."

The conferee declared: "I have considered myself quite conscious of denominational differences, but now I see that through Christ it's really just one family. Doctrine is secondary; the power of Christ to change a man is primary. Well, my cup is so full I'm just amazed. This world and all its cares are so dim. I believe God wanted me to be at that conference, and had I not made it—well, it frightens me.

"My own experience," he continued, "has been so up and down, and mostly down, under various pressures and weakness of the flesh, but now I see that one can have spiritual bones which will not be shaken. Pray for me to go forward and to start all over. I was a fighter, but as I knelt He so quickly forgave and the world never looked sweeter. But when real pressures and tests came, I didn't hold up too well, although much better than before. But you see what Cannon Beach has done for me!"

Many lives have been transformed as a result of these weekend meetings. Unbelievers have faced their Maker; believers have had their lives revived.

CHAPTER SIXTEEN

TOP PRIORITY

"How important it is that every business and professional man be a constant, consistent witness! May we be as faithful satellites and stars - reflecting the Son of God that others might see the light." - Andrew W. Hughes, comptroller, Rheem Manufacturing Company, New York City, N. Y.

IN CHRISTIAN BUSINESS MEN'S BUSINESS COMMITTEE INTERNATIONAL, 1954 was another year of miracles. In Eugene, Oregon, for example, two CBMC men—business competitors across the street from each other—became burdened for the spiritual needs of the city. Herb Jauchenmen's clothier, later vice-president of Westmont College, Santa Barbara, California—and Fred Rady, shoe merchant, agreed to pray together for God to satisfy those needs.

They summed up their feelings in this maxim: "When you rely on entertainment, you get what entertainment can do; when you rely on personalities, you get what personalities can do; but when you rely on prayer, you get what God will do."

Believing that implicitly, the two men started early Tuesday morning prayer periods. Beginning with a mere handful, the prayer periods soon began to attract forty to fifty men each week. Encouragement came from time to time in miraculous answers to prayer. A monthly CBMC dinner meeting began with sixty-six men and a great deal of enthusiasm. The first anniversary banquet brought out six hundred persons to hear Waldo Yeager. Laymen and pastors alike recognized God's hand working in Eugene.

Dr. Vance Webster, pastor of the First Baptist Church, declared that "the pastors of the fundamental churches of Eugene are grateful for CBMC and its new life and power for God in our community."

One could never pinpoint God's method of working at a given time or in a given place. "God works in mysterious ways His wonders to perform." That was never more true than in the ministry of CBMC, as the front-page story in the Pembroke (Ontario) *Standard-Observer* proves.

Two would-be robbers, Ross Lloyd and Normand Gauthier, hungry and desperate, had come into Pembroke to "case" a jewelry store for a planned robbery. A poster caught their eyes. CBMC was sponsoring speaker Jim Vaus, former gangster turned evangelist. They went in and heard the speaker's message on "Why I Quit Syndicated Crime." Both made a profession of faith in Christ.

At about the same time, in another part of the continent, God moved in a mysterious way. A fifty-two-year-old Californian, a drunkard for eleven years, picked up a copy of Waldo Yeager's tract entitled "Life's Most Amazing Fact." The message he read helped influence the ex-drunkard to commit his life to God. "It was the happiest and surely the most exciting time of my life," he said, "when I said 'Yes' to Jesus Christ. Boy! I know now it's truly 'life's most amazing fact.'"

God's men of CBMC had not exhausted His unusual ways of working. On a plane to Washington, D.C., one Sunday morning, two Christian business men proved themselves alert to opportunity. G. Tom Willey, vice-president and general manager of The Martin Company, Orlando, Florida, and Robert P. Woodburn, vice-president of The National Bank of Washington, D.C., were flying from a speaking appointment in the East. Suddenly they realized it was time for Sunday morning worship service.

Without embarrassment, they asked the captain for permission to conduct a brief service over the loudspeaker. Approval granted, they explained to the startled passengers what they intended to do. Then each man spoke briefly of his faith in God. They read from the Bible, then handed out small leaflets containing personal testimonies of other persons.

With only one exception, the passengers received the leaflets gladly. Alighting from the plane, Willey and Woodburn were stopped by the pilot. He grasped their hands, expressing his personal thanks for conducting the service.

The two men had worked to meet the demands made of CBMC men. Arnold Grunigen had written twelve points showing the demands made by the CBMC movement:

1. "Christian Business Men's Committee operates that we might tackle men of our size for the Gospel. It trains us, as witnessing Christians, to think—which is so hard, before we act—which is so easy.

2. "CBMC is not formed to indulge our appetites to feed our fancy with strange doctrines, peculiar twistings of scripture truth, or fanciful views of the same. We forget some of the timeworn phrases; we pass over some of the old forms; we re-express its convictions, we restate them to fit the times in which we find ourselves. We are not bound by theological language which has been approved by the seal of approval agencies. We do not have to have a ready-made vocabulary that has been approved in high places. Thank God!

3. "This is no grouping for dull or unreflecting men who are full of inertia. We welcome change. We are interested in ideas and plans to be used in aggressive evangelism. This operation is not tradition-bound. It enjoys thoughtfully-planned innovations. It is a menace to permanence. It is a training, testing and developing agency for aggressive laymen. It is not a mass movement; it is an operation by a specialist grouping.

4. "It knows that there are great forces in Heaven and earth that man's philosophy cannot fathom; it does not trust human reason, and it has great faith in God's prescription.

5. "It does not smile at flights of eloquent, windy oratory. It dearly loves pungent, meaningful, clipped sentences from warm hearts of believing men. It has eliminated political expediency from its usual high place in organizational efforts.

6. "It matures and instructs, until it cuts down and reduces and affects control of the following very serious ailments in the body of Christ: pride, ambition, avarice, revenge, lust, sedition, hypocrisy, ungoverned zeal, disorderly appetites in its membership. It makes for disciplined men. It reduces the velocity of the storms enumerated above that constantly trouble life.

7. "It is a vehicle that provides reason for performing what we consider our duty and privilege. Membership obviously exposes us to work, sacrifices of comfort; but it causes us to aim for and achieve targets that are otherwise unrealized.

8. "It has taken a living faith that was often trudging down the trail, often reposing on the shelf in good condition, polished it, brightened it, to make it really live in hearts, lives and testimonies. It's made Christianity, salvation, and kindred subjects easy to talk about. It multiplied conversations and contacts, it has cut down hesitation and ambiguities in our approach with the Gospel.

9. "It has been a vital aid in 'putting first things first'; spreading the Gospel has top priority with us. This life-giving recipe is not just a social type to be used in times of national or international emergency.

10. "It has strengthened and bulwarked us against the perplexities that newspapers and radios deluge us with, not to mention the conundrum and the riddle of atomic energy, new weapons of war, success or failure of international organizations, and the menace of Russian power. It has delivered us from much uncertainty, because we live and

work not for this world, and we know what we believe.

11. "It supplies hope for a decent, tranquil, prospering state amid a muddled world scene. It causes us to be able to meet nearly any temporary exigency. Men ignorant of final causes could not meet or answer these so well.

12. "Finally, Christian Business Men's Committee has really helped in saving us from a crass and a vulgar economy in our various placements of life. We budget our time and strength. Cheap substitutes for real life and living have less appeal. We have experienced the 'much mores' of the Word. The world seems dedicated to the short-run. Under God, and with His help, every day finds us laying plans for the long-run. Tried with like passions, tested in a similar manner, this happy, voluntary, unusual aggregation of twice-born men has declared dividends since the company was first organized. Holy Spirit direction is constantly coveted, that there may be no letdown until the 'upper-taker' calls."

Another international leader, T. E. McCully, keynoted the Los Angeles convention with reasons for the existence of CBMC.

"We are not here to duplicate the work of the Bible-believing church," he declared. "We believe in rendering the fullest cooperation to our local church or assembly. We are not here to be a sponsoring organization. I believe first of all God has called us as individuals into this CBMC fellowship to present a forceful testimony to the men whom we contact every day in our particular line of business."

McCully cautioned against a weak approach to the task at hand. "We are not to be wishy-washy about this," he said, "but strong, using every opportunity, realizing that we can never speak to the wrong man about Christ. We need encouragement and help from each other and so we meet in weekly luncheons and prayer groups to stimulate and encourage victorious testimony."

Continual burnishing and inspiration from leaders such as Grunigen and McCully influenced local members of Christian Business Men's Committees to rally to the cause. In Lakewood, California, for example, the CBMC of Long Beach sponsored a three-week evangelistic campaign with Dr. Merv Rosell. During the three weeks, 1,088 persons made commitments to Christ.

In Kansas City, Missouri, CBMC men conducted a service at the United States Disciplinary Barracks in Leavenworth, Kansas. A hundred weeping prisoners came up to the altar. Similar services have been held in numerous jails, prisons and penitentiaries across the continent.

Prisoners are only one target for the CBMC witness of business and professional men. The CBMC of Lansing, Michigan, co-sponsored a booth with Youth for Christ at the Ingham County Fair in Mason, Michigan. For a week Youth for Christ and CBMC men distributed tracts, talked personally to interested passersby, and gave flannelgraph demonstrations for children. The net result: 140 decisions for Christ.

The individual continued to play a most important part in CBMC. In the Pacific Northwest, a prosecuting attorney attended his first CBMC meeting in February, 1954.

"Seven years ago, as County Prosecuting Attorney," declared Robert E. Conner of Wenatchee, Washington, "I really had the tables turned on me. A young man against whom I had issued a criminal warrant for the crime of grand larceny, and of whom I even suspected murder, sat across the desk and asked me a personal question that put me on the spot."

For four years, the FBI had searched for this man, Conner pointed out. One day the man turned himself in to the Chief of Detectives of the city of Portland, who in turn called Conner. The man quietly but boldly queried the prosecuting attorney.

"Mr. Conner," he asked, "are you a Christian?"

"Sure," Conner replied simply. "I'm a member of the church."

"Have you been born again?" the man persisted.

"I'm a deacon in the church," Connor replied. "What do you mean by being born again?"

The ex-fugitive opened his Bible and explained the new birth to the attorney, not pressing him for a decision. Conner felt tremendously relieved when the man left.

Shortly after this conversation, Conner attended the men's retreat for his church. "I was a good attender at these," he said, "really anxious to receive something real, but never finding it. As a church officer and prominent official, I was to give the main morning message. My recent conversation and a few CBMC friends had convinced me that a man didn't have to go on sinning. I determined to speak on that subject. But I had nothing to give.

"On the Friday before the retreat," Conner continued, "a strange thing happened. When I returned from court, even my secretary couldn't account for a book that had been left on my desk. It was an old book, but one that had never been used. Even the pages had to be cut apart at the edge. In the middle was a pamphlet dividing the book at a chapter that began with a verse from the Bible: 'What shall we say then? Shall we continue to sin that grace may abound? God forbid' (Romans 6:1)."

More than a year later, Conner said, he learned that a Christian woman had been led to pray for him. She had sent the book to his office and had placed the pamphlet inside it.

"In that book by James McConkey," Conner said, "my questions about sin were fully answered. Even so, however, I became more miserable the closer it came to the hour of the retreat. I felt about like a man would feel if he had to drive a railroad spike with a feather hammer. The burden was overwhelming. I left an earlier meeting and went off alone to try to pray about the matter."

Conner knelt as he had seen CBMC men do. When someone approached, he felt ashamed to be seen praying. "Right then and there," he said, "God revealed to me the awful disgrace of my pride. The testimonies and the Word swept over me, and I saw Christ—'high and lifted up.'

"I saw the blows that fell," he continued. "I saw the blood run down. I saw the sinless perfection and beauty, marred and destroyed for my sins. The rest of the world was swept away. There at the foot of the cross I wept and confessed and repented, and my sins 'which were many'—were all washed away. I knew that I was saved. Not only the converted criminal, but also others had had a vital part in delivering me from churchianity and introducing me to real Christianity, which is centered in the person of Christ."

As County Prosecuting Attorney in 1949, Conner had been asked to investigate a youth prayer meeting held at noon in the home of a schoolteacher. It was suspected that the activity might be subversive or communistic. Conner found the leader of the group to be his high school mathematics teacher. Her high character during those high school years made it impossible for Conner to question her conduct.

Then Conner began to notice newspaper ads about Youth for Christ (YFC) meetings. "Surely these will need investigation," he thought. "If they were really Christian, they'd be church sponsored."

"At that time," Conner said, "the YFC director himself began to contact me and urged me to attend meetings of a new organization called the Christian Business Men's Committee. Through his dogged persistence, I finally attended my first CBMC meeting. This was in February of 1954. There I heard men testify of their salvation—a word I had never even heard before, despite my being a deacon in the church and a Sunday school teacher.

"'These men really have something,' I said to another one of our church officers who had attended. Their expressions and comments reflected confidence, joy and deep peace—something for which I really longed. No one offended me by inquiry about my personal state. All I saw was kindness, sincerity and welcome. It was so genuine that I didn't miss a chance to attend their other meetings. Then I was invited to attend a CBMC conference at Cannon Beach, Oregon, four hundred miles away."

Though he thought it impossible and ridiculous, Conner decided to go. Arriving late at night with his wife and four young children, Conner saw the local CBMC chairman standing out in the rain waiting for him.

"Soon we were registered and lodged," Conner continued. "And thus, through simple kindness and generosity, began a memorable weekend of fellowship, testimony, and preaching. I remember saying to my wife on the way home, 'I feel as if I've had a brainwashing'—so refreshing that conference was.

"Then came the experience with the converted criminal," Conner continued, "which God used as another stepping stone for me to Himself. After my salvation, my rejoicing was so extreme that I had to tell everyone. My joy was so great that I couldn't seem to get my feet down on the sidewalk."

The following few years were not fruitful in winning souls, Conner admitted, but the conditioning was under way. "Things did begin to work," he said, "when I finally learned it was 'not by might, nor by power, but by my Spirit, saith the Lord.' Since then, the Lord has been so kind to let me see my whole family and my law partner in the fold, one by one.

"I praise Him daily for the 'so great a cloud of witnesses' with which He surrounded me and for the Christian Business Men's Committee. Through the CBMC I first heard the Gospel, and through CBMC I find the major drive and inspiration for my life and business today."

CHAPTER SEVENTEEN

NEW CREATIONS

"Any Christian, regardless of his vocation, who is not actively involved in the task of sharing Christ with his fellowmen, has broken his contract of service. He is out on strike against God." – Howard Butt, Jr., Corpus Christi, Texas, grocery executive

IN CHRISTIAN BUSINESS MEN'S BUSINESS COMMITTEE INTERNATIONAL, the year 1955 marked the end of one era and the beginning of another.

Donald MacDonald, at retirement age and not in good health, tendered his resignation as executive secretary. The Board of Directors set out to find a replacement under whom the steady growth of the movement would continue. Retiring International Chairman T. E. McCully, whose three-year term as a director expired at the 1955 convention in Washington, D.C., had felt God lead him away from the baking business. He had felt the urgency of the hour and the great potential of business and professional men on the firing line for God. He had already aroused many men to their responsibilities and privileges as witnesses.

After much prayer, McCully accepted the appointment of the board to replace MacDonald as executive secretary. The official date of transfer was January 1, 1956. McCully came into the international office several weeks early in order that he and MacDonald might effect a smooth transition.

In his year as international chairman, McCully had visited sixty committees. He had attended four regional conferences and two retreats. God had graciously prepared him for his ministry in the international office.

A New York-California executive became the new international chairman. Richard Woike commuted between his investment firm in New York City and the Houston-Fearless Corporation in West Los Angeles, of which he was board chairman. His oratorical achievements at times bordered on brilliance. A convention message in Phoenix, Arizona, brought so much response that the American Tract Society printed the speech in booklet form. It became a top seller. Woike called his allegory, "The Chevrolet That Wanted to Be a Cadillac."

With the conclusion of the address in Phoenix, Woike issued a simple appeal for any who might be interested in making a commitment to Christ. The audience had heard clearly what happens when a man yields himself to the Lord. Twelve or more men in the audience responded to Woike's appeal.

CHAPTER EIGHTEEN

FALLEN GIANTS

"And I sought for a man among them, that should make up the hedge, and stand in the gap before me for the land, that I should not destroy it: but I found none" (Ezekiel 22:30).

ON THE EIGHTEENTH OF JANUARY, 1956, Arnold Grunigen, Jr. went to his reward. Ten days earlier, five young missionaries in the jungles of Ecuador met death at the hands of Auca Indians.

One of them was Ed McCully, the son of CBMCI Executive Secretary T. E. McCully. Sober reflection and heartfelt sympathy characterized the entire movement this first month in 1956. Grunigen had packed a lifetime of vibrant Christianity into his compressed fifty-four years previous to a series of illnesses and operations. On Sunday morning just three days before his death, he had addressed a capacity crowd of 150 people gathered in the Fireside room of the Peninsula Bible Church in Palo Alto. It was his final message in a series of three.

"Heaven is the goal and hope of the believer," he began. "The unsaved person is spending his time, effort and money on earthly habitations. Suppose there was a chance that you could live to be 104, like the man I heard of over in Berkeley who just recently went home to glory. I'm not saying that you will, understand, but just suppose you did."

The nature of his remarks caused many to wonder if Grunigen perhaps had a premonition of his early fate. "None of us knows how long we are going to be able to hold out," he declared. "As I look you over this morning, I am not good enough to tell whether you will last that long or not and you're not good enough to say whether you'll last that long. I don't know, but even if you did live that long, what is that compared with eternity? Spending eternity with Him will be the most glorious thing for the believer.

"When the body returns to dust," Grunigen continued, "and it will if the Lord tarries, then comes the house not made with hands. We, the believers that is, are clothed by God. Paul's immortal hope of glory will be the personal experience of one Arnold Grunigen. I don't know why it is, but we hang on to this life even though we are looking forward to being clothed."

Near the end of his message, Grunigen said, "We must be willing to be absent from the body and to be present with the Lord." Just at this point his physical difficulties made it hard for him to continue. Several times he repeated the words—"absent . . . present . . . it's terrific. I'll be there." Within fifty-four hours after his final message, Arnold Grunigen had died.

His close personal friend, Bob LeTourneau, remarked: "We will miss him, but God will give him a good job in Heaven, because He has found him dependable."

T. E. McCully, hiding a broken heart and using Christian service to compensate for the loss of his son, began a never-ending schedule of speaking assignment, office duties, and extra-curricular activities. His only explanation for the extra physical reserve that belied his near-retirement age was: "They that wait upon the Lord shall renew their strength" (Isaiah 40:31).

Day after day, week after week, month after month—with rarely even a weekend respite—McCully maintained a schedule too rigorous for many a younger man. As long as he saw spiritual results continue to accrue obviously and readily to him, the baking executive would not slow down. In June of 1956, Wheaton College (Illinois) awarded McCully an honorary Doctor of Laws degree.

God continued to honor the faithful testimony of laymen. In Charleston, West Virginia, for example, CBMC member Maynard Davis invited the Superintendent of Parks and Recreation, Robert Kresge, to a Christian Business Men's Committee luncheon.

"I enjoyed the friendliness of the men," Kresge said, "and did

not think their talks and testimonies too strange, so I attended
for several weeks in succession. A few weeks before Easter, I
remembered something we had done back in Butler, Pennsylvania, with considerable success. I had hoped to introduce it in
Charleston, but had met with little enthusiasm on the part of
prospective sponsors."

The YMCA in Butler had sponsored a Good Friday men's
breakfast. Kresge thought the CBMC of Charleston would take
hold of his idea. "Although the time was short," he said, "the
men did take on the project—mainly, I learned later, for the sake
of my own spiritual welfare. The time was to be at 6:30 A.M.
on Good Friday, at a local restaurant, with a Winston-Salem car
dealer, Matt Howell, as speaker. I was not a CBMC member,
but I worked with the other men on the breakfast, selling tickets
and handling publicity. About 130 men overflowed the room.
Several inquiries followed the Gospel message by Howell."

After the breakfast, Kresge drove Matt Howell around town.
They stopped at the home of Harry Musser, Jr., a leader in the
CBMC of Charleston. "There," Kresge said, "Matt confronted
me with my own spiritual condition. I admitted a lack in my
life, and he read to me from the Bible. 'That if thou shalt confess
with thy mouth the Lord Jesus, and shalt believe in thine heart
that God hath raised him from the dead, thou shalt be saved. For
with the heart man believeth unto righteousness; and with the
mouth confession is made unto salvation' (Romans 10:9,10).

"There in the living room," Kresge said, "I confessed Jesus
Christ as my own personal Saviour. The project I had suggested
had been God's means, eventually, of bringing me to Himself."

Experiences such as the experience of Kresge began to occur
with such frequency that Richard Woike evolved an idea. He
thought of devoting special issues of the official publication,
CBMC Contact, to these testimonies exclusively. The "house
organ" material could be relegated to other issues. His idea met
with resounding approval, and February, June and September

issues each year thereafter became Personal Experience Issues. Scores of men ordered bulk quantities for distribution at doctor and dentist offices, barber shops, libraries, jails, hospitals, and other places. The stories of spiritual rebirth stirred many hearts. Another witnessing medium for CBMC had been born.

In employing a variety of media, the CBMCI used the nine-point Statement of Doctrine as a balance wheel to keep the movement on a steady course.

CHAPTER NINETEEN

SECRET OF SUCCESS

"God has left us down here to shine. We are not here to buy and sell and get gain, to accumulate wealth, to acquire worldly position. This earth, if we are Christians, is not our home; it is up yonder."
– Dwight L. Moody, founder of Moody Bible Institute, Chicago

SLOW BUT STEADY GROWTH continued to mark the Christian Business Men's Committee International in 1957. Waldo Yeager succeeded Richard Woike as international chairman. Scores of speaking engagements and counseling sessions in all parts of the United States and Canada marked his busy tenure at the top of the organizational ladder.

In 1958, A. Reid Jepson, nephew of CBMCI co-founder Dr. N. A. Jepson, assumed duties as special representative, working out of Charleston, West Virginia. Especially in the Southeast, Jepson was used to spur existing committees and to establish new groups. He also helped to plan, promote, and actually conduct Christian Business Men's Crusades.

Such lay crusades really came of age in 1958. In August of that year, the small town of New Bern, North Carolina, first tasted genuine revival—a city-wide atmosphere of Divine Presence manifested in diverse ways.

A year earlier, furniture dealer Ernest Smith had made a covenant with God. Feeling he had wasted most of his fifty years, he wanted the rest of his life to count for eternity. He began with a spiritual awakening in his home town. He began to pray, and soon others joined him. The newly-formed Christian Business Men's Committee of New Bern, headed by Smith, went to work.

Early in the year they planned a Christian Business Men's Crusade—normally a nine-day lay campaign beginning on a Saturday night. The campaign included testimonies of business and professional men. A Winston-Salem car dealer, Matt Howell, later in church financing at Waynesville, North Carolina, met with Vernon W. Patterson, retired from Moore Forms, Inc., Charlotte, North Carolina. They conferred about speakers to lead in the campaign.

Meanwhile, prayer saturation continued. New Bern men sought and found open doors in numerous offices, plants and shops. Managers agreed to allow early morning prayer time for interested employees. Enthusiasm and excitement increased as the crusade opening date approached.

Speakers, business men and professional men, flying in from various parts of the country, reported that they sensed a Divine Presence even as they landed in the North Carolina town. It seemed strangely easy to talk about spiritual matters on the streets, in drugstores and restaurants.

"The Spirit of God was beginning to move on the entire city," Howell said. "People were easy to win to the Lord Jesus Christ. On one occasion I was asked to visit two men who had a personal grievance between them. Both Christians, they had not spoken to each other in years. They were confronted with this sin in their lives and prayed with individually.

"These two men," Howell continued, "confessed their sin, shook hands, and later publicly stood together on the crusade platform as an indication of their reconciliation."

Howell added that "we saw a mighty outpouring of God's Spirit in the downtown area, and the store owners and managers were more than willing to have revival among the employees. We were at liberty to do personal work in the restaurants, department stores, drugstores, and elsewhere, as the entire town was talking about the Crusade. By this time you could hardly find a person who had not attended at least one rally. The entire city was in an atmosphere of revival."

The president of the New Bern Ministerial Association, the Reverend Cecil H. Campbell, said: "This has been one of the most amazing workings of the Holy Spirit that I have experienced in the twenty-seven years of my Gospel ministry. I cannot evaluate the results of such a crusade too highly. It is nothing short of a modern day miracle."

The crusade in North Carolina became the springboard for many similarly blessed crusades. None of the subsequent crusades, however, seemed as gloriously eventful as the crusade in New Bern.

The balance between *doing* and *being* continued as leaders sounded the need for men to take in and be before they attempt to give out and do. One of the leaders sounding this need was George D. Armerding, an Oakland, California, food manufacturing equipment executive.

"How do we as Christian business men measure up to God's standard of perfection?" he asked. "More and more in these days of automation, we demand perfection. When we dial a phone call, we expect the number that we dialed to answer us. When we stop for gasoline, we expect the pump to put as much gasoline in the tank as is indicated by the figures showing the amount delivered."

Armerding added that "when we climb aboard an airplane, anything short of perfection of the equipment would be unthinkable. From the smallest item of our demands to the largest, we expect perfection.

"Conversely," he continued, "when we appraise our own abilities, we pass off perfection as simply unattainable. Yet, as we study our Bible, we find that God has demanded perfection from our forebears and He demands it from us."

With such stirring exhortations from its leaders, Christian Business Men's Committee International continued to expand its ministry into all corners of the world. In Toronto a CBMC booth at the Canadian National Exhibition brought sixty-four commitments to Christ as business and professional men talked with interested passersby. Some eighty thousand Gospel tracts went out from the booth.

In New York City, another former international chairman achieved his "promotion." Baking executive Robert S. Swanson celebrated Christmas Day by playing with his grandchildren. Suddenly he fell over, victim of a heart attack. T. E. McCully and many other Christian leaders flew to his funeral.

Dr. V. Raymond Edman, president of Wheaton College, said of him: "Bob Swanson was one of the greatest Christians I have ever known. He was energetic, enthusiastic, untiring in the Lord's work. He carried large administrative responsibilities in his business, but he always had time for fellowship with the Lord's people, for prayer with someone in need, for a word of encouragement to one of his men.

"Bob had a burden of heart for the salvation of others. When passing through a city he would pray for the governor, mayor, policemen and other officials. When some need was mentioned, his immediate response would be, 'Let's pray about that right now.' Life has been sweeter because of him, and heaven greatly to be desired."

The first Canadian to serve as chairman of Christian Business Men's Committee International was Donald F. McKechnie, an Ottawa, Ontario, accounting executive who served faithfully and zealously in 1958. He visited scores of committees in the United States and Canada, and the movement continued to grow under his astute leadership.

As always, Canadians played an extremely vital part in the overall program of CBMCI. Annually, some 500 or more Christian business men from the provinces meet together at Canadian Keswick for the Eastern Canada Regional Conference, truly a glorious time of fellowship and blessing.

With the year's end, CBMCI began to make plans for outreach into other lands on a greater scale than ever before. The work in foreign countries had been plainly fragmentary. A renewed interest promised increased witnessing of business and professional men abroad.

CHAPTER TWENTY

TO THE UTTERMOST PARTS

"We have reached an hour in the history of civilization which I believe is one of the most crucial mankind has ever been called upon to face."
— Hon. Ernest C. Manning, Premier of Alberta, Canada

ON THE NATIONAL SCENE, IN 1959, Hawaii became our fiftieth state, and Christian A. Herter succeeded John Foster Dulles as Secretary of State. The television quiz scandals attested to moral decay in the nation's fabric. The time was ripe for renewed spiritual appeals. CBMC pledged itself anew to the task.

Steady growth of the movement had led to more than 450 committees in the United States, Canada and thirty other countries. Revealing a new emphasis on foreign expansion, the Board of Directors unanimously and enthusiastically approved a trip to the far east by executive secretary McCully and Director J. Elliott Stedelbauer. As with all such trips, directors and other local CBMC leaders traveled at their own expense.

In Manila, at the beginning of their tour, McCully and Stedelbauer heard a missionary say she had gone to the mission field after God spoke to her through the martyrdom of the five missionaries in Ecuador. In Bangkok, the travelers found a former chairman of the CBMC of Buffalo, New York. The former chairman, Les Chopard, had become a missionary in Laos.

"The thing that impressed us," McCully said, "as we went from one large city to another was the untold millions who are still untold. We visited some of the famous Buddhist temples and saw the people bowing down to Buddha, burning incense before him and making their wishes."

Kenneth Wong, Youth for Christ director in Calcutta, India, took the two men on a tour of Calcutta. "Again our hearts were moved as we saw the Hindus sacrificing to their gods and goddesses," McCully said. "We were taken down to the Ganges river and watched the people trying to wash away their sins.

"Then," he continued, "we went to the temple where the people were killing goats for sacrifices in order to appease their gods and goddesses. The sights were amazing and almost unbelievable. We were taken to another place where the people burn the dead bodies. They had just put a baby's body on the fire. All the Hindus cremate the dead. Then they put the ashes on a boat and scatter them on the Ganges river."

At the Madras airport, about fifty CBMC men from Madras and Gummidipundi welcomed the two travelers. Alighting at the same time, visiting Willy Brandt, Mayor of West Berlin, expressed surprise at the warm reception until he realized it was not for him.

In Melbourne, Australia, Stedelbauer and McCully visited with Dr. Billy Graham during the closing days of his crusade in that city. Some 143,000 people—then a record attendance for a single Graham Crusade meeting—overflowed Melbourne Cricket Grounds on Sunday, March 15, the final meeting.

In New Zealand, the two men found a warm welcome and made new friends for CBMC. Before the two-month tour ended, several new committees had been formed.

CHAPTER TWENTY-ONE

A BREATH OF HEAVEN

"The key to CBMC moving forward rests, not in avenues or devices, not in more salaried personnel, but in dedicated, born again business men giving their personal witness each day to the business world."
— G. Tom Willey, vice-president and general manager,
The Martin Company, Orlando, Florida

IN 1960, THE TOTAL NUMBER of committees finally reached the five hundred mark. Harry R. Smith, vice-president and Chicago representative of the Bank of America, became international chairman; James E. Colville, vice-president of John Adams Henry Corp., a produce firm, New York, New York, vice-chairman; R. G. LeTourneau, vice-chairman; Secretary G. Tom Willey; and Treasurer Aaron Denlinger, a lumber, feed, and coal executive, Paradise, Pennsylvania.

Despite a brief period of sickness that hampered his activities, Chairman Smith provided capable leadership and met with committees throughout the continent. In Mount Vernon, Washington, an evangelistic campaign scheduled for eight days extended to five weeks. Revival rocked the area under the spiritual ministry of Dr. Torrey Johnson and Hilding Halvarson. More than four hundred commitments to Christ in the CBMC-sponsored campaign included Mayor Donald Lindblom and his family. The entire town of Mount Vernon, and surrounding towns, felt the impact of the campaign.

A Baptist pastor in Hartselle, Alabama, responded to several articles he had been reading, articles about the revival in New Bern, North Carolina. Three participants in the New Bern crusade flew to Hartselle for an Inter-Church Meeting for Spiritual Awakening. More than 1400 persons attended the Sunday afternoon session. Ninety persons responded to a Gospel invitation at the close of the meeting.

Hartselle ministers and laymen planned an eight-day crusade similar to the crusade in New Bern. God did send a measure of revival to Hartselle, as indicated by more than a hundred and fifty commitments.

One pastor said, "There is an unmistakably evident increase of interest in spiritual and eternal issues among a number of people here since the crusade. It seems probable that the crusade has produced the beginning of the spiritual awakening that has been prayed for here."

Aided by Special Representative Reid Jepson, the laymen active in the Hartselle Crusade formed a Christian Business Men's Committee a few days after the crusade. Editor Jack Hoffhaus of *The Hartselle Inquirer* became the committee chairman. Associate Editor Sam Houston, skeptical of the crusade until he too responded to the call for commitment one night, wrote in his "Small Voice" column:

"We applaud the beginning of the group of dedicated Christian men, whose efforts can now be concentrated and directed to purposeful ends. We believe the things that may be wrought by them here will have eternal consequences."

CBMC did not neglect the newly-discovered fields abroad. Early in 1960, six CBMC leaders traveled in twenty countries of Europe: Chairman Waldo Yeager; Vice-Chairman Robert Kellogg, Sacramento, California, pharmacy owner; Dr. Ross Willows, Winnipeg, Manitoba, obstetrician and gynecologist, a former CBMCI director; David Redekop, also of Winnipeg, owner of an electrical firm and also a former CBMCI director; Stedelbauer; and McCully. A number of new committees resulted, including Aberdeen and Glasgow, Scotland.

Finding a warm Christian welcome wherever they went, the six CBMC travelers were greatly strengthened and encouraged in their task of stimulating business and professional men to a more faithful witness of their spiritual beliefs. In turn, the tiny acorns of faith they planted could be used of God to become giant oaks.

On the home front, the executive committee of Fishers of Men, Inc.—outgrowth of the earlier Billy Sunday Clubs in the Southern States—appointed President Ted DeMoss, a Chattanooga insurance executive, to investigate the possibility of merging with CBMCI. After a conference with McCully, DeMoss accepted an invitation to present the proposed merger to the CBMCI Board in convention at Seattle.

After a series of negotiations, the merger took effect and the Fishers of Men officially became a part of the larger movement. Former leaders of the F.O.M. assumed duties as regional counselors for CBMCI and began to work in their new assignments.

That step of unity in the ranks of interdenominational organizations helped to cement the entire membership in a new way. Christian business and professional men approached their tasks with renewed vigor.

CHAPTER TWENTY-TWO

A PUBLISHER CONFESSES

"What we are talking about is not a human struggle of self-effort for holiness. It is not Christian character manufactured by dint of human prowess. Here is a work of the Holy Ghost that comes to pass when first of all there is death."
— Dr. William Culbertson, president, Moody Bible Institute, Chicago.

AMID EXCITING HEADLINES of one Russian space flight and two American space flights, Christian Business Men's Committee International moved forward in 1961 under the chairmanship of a Williamsport, Pennsylvania, attorney, Alfred R. Jackson. His duties carried him into various parts of the continent. A California publisher made his own headlines after his first brush with a California CBMC.

Don C. Matchan, editor and publisher of Herald of Health, a monthly San Francisco periodical, carried an unusual editorial in his magazine.

"Normally," he wrote, "this space is reserved for the editor's comment, for whatever it may or may not be worth, on issues and developments in the field of health.

"However, on this occasion I am going to use whatever space is required to 'bare my soul,' so to speak—and to 'witness' in behalf of the Christ, Jesus, through whom I have been privileged to glimpse the wonders of an existence touched by the Holy Spirit, Hand of God, or whatever you wish to call it.

"I am deeply grateful for the privilege of having been led down this path—actually the result of being 'worked on' by a long-time friend, Postmaster P. W. Helena of Los Altos, California, an organizer of the Christian Business Men's Committee of the Peninsula Area in California.

"The steps involved," editor Matchan continued, "in going from a casually interested—and shall we say 'sympathetically tolerant' attitude—to the hour of 'decision' are not important, except to me. Suffice to say, I had resisted a full acknowledgment of the power and place of the spiritual for many years. Yes, I'm a 'good' Episcopalian, but have contributed little beyond limited financial aid - to the well-being or progress of the church.

"I have been a proud person with a strong ego complex. To ask help has been distasteful; to admit that I needed help—and that it could come only from the source of the infinite—was a step I could not bring myself to make. I delved into the meta-physical and still believe it has its place, though perhaps not the be-all and end-all to human problems.

"I used to think of my postmaster friend as a 'fundamentalist.' His views amused me, and I thought, 'the poor guy, he is so primitive in his thinking. He is short on intellectual capacity.'

"Indeed," Matchan continued, "as it appears to me now, this attitude was a result of a lack of humility on my part. Today I believe intellectual achievement and humility and God-con-sciousness, or whatever you want to call it, go hand in hand.

"It was not easy—and I did it somewhat abashedly—to tell my wife that I had 'accepted Christ,' following one of a series of evening meetings of the previously mentioned Christian Business Men's Committee. (For years I had avoided contact with that group because I had believed, utterly without foundation, that it was anti-Semitic and if so, I could have no part in it. Actually, it is made up of intelligent, cultured men in all the professions, from art to law and medicine, as well as leading businessmen.)"

The publisher admitted that "I have always been an 'inde-pendent' spirit, more or less, and somehow the idea of devotion to certain of the Biblical precepts seemed to me to show lack of moral fiber, weakness of a sort. (Though the Golden Rule and brother's-keeper philosophy I accepted almost fiercely.)

"I can say now, however," Matchan continued, "that to publicly acclaim Christ as Saviour—to walk down an aisle with many persons looking on and to ask admittance to the sanctum of Christ's saving grace—requires 'independence' and conviction.

"I can say now that each day I experience a quiet—and sometimes exhilarating—feeling of genuine joy that this decision has been made. And I find myself hungry for information about the experiences of those of His day, and earlier, who carried the torch — so I read the Bible, almost avidly, and pray that I shall grow in knowledge. And in works.

"And I write this with the knowledge that some may exclaim, 'Has Matchan lost his marbles?' And some may feel sorry for me. I made a vow to myself, in accepting Christ completely, that I would have no shame about union with Him. Since the Lord has given me stewardship over this magazine, to use these columns as I see fit—I feel a deep compulsion to discuss this thing with all who will read, as is done herein. And having done—a sense of satisfaction comes over me. And I am grateful for the opportunity.

"P.S. I hope this will not be interpreted as implying that suddenly I have no charity for any except 'Christians.' On the other hand, my respect and love for other humans, regardless of their training or beliefs, has increased, if anything. And I shall rejoice if, along the road, I may help one or many come to know the peace, the joy, the strength which they can have simply by unlocking their hearts and inviting the Holy Spirit in."

Testimonies like these strengthened the entire membership and lent inexpressible encouragement to pursue the spiritual warfare.

At the year's end, a four-man team flew to South America to augment the movement's Operation Outreach. Accompanying Executive Secretary McCully were Herbert Frybarger, Oakland, California, insurance executive; Ernest Matthias, Jr., Waterloo, Iowa, president of a dredging firm; and Elliott Stedelbauer, 1962 ambassador-at-large for CBMCI by virtue of a board appointment at the Montreal convention. More than a hundred commitments of faith resulted from the trip, and at least twenty-three prospective Christian Business Men's Committees emerged.

CHAPTER TWENTY-THREE

RIPE FRUIT IN THE SOUTH

"All that the Church and its members need for the manifestation of the mighty power of God in the world is the return to our true place, the place that belongs to us, both in creation and redemption, the place of absolute and unceasing dependence upon God." – Andrew Murray

THE NAME OF COL. JOHN GLENN led all the rest as 1962 made its grand entrance on the stage of history. His three-orbital flight around the world stirred the imagination of Americans. Khrushchev eased the pressure in Berlin and other strategic points, but the cold war nevertheless continued. President Kennedy blasted the steel industry for its price increase, and three days later it rescinded the increase.

Meanwhile, a former professional hockey player, Andrew W. Hughes, later comptroller for the Rheem Manufacturing Company, New York, New York, held the reins of the thriving CBMCI movement. His energetic leadership brought a forward advance felt in many of the world's areas. No spectacular growth marked the period, but the same steady, substantial expansion added impetus to the new spiritual strides achieved.

More and more, the leadership of CBMCI stressed quality as opposed to mere quantity. Nevertheless, the need for additional "lay mission stations" in towns and cities all over America and the world remained critical. Harbingers of national revival, a condition greatly desired by the movement's leaders, erupted in at least two areas in the South.

In February, simultaneous Christian Business Men's Crusades in Lakeland and Winter Haven, Florida, brought almost all the people in the area the message of the Gospel. Huge billboards, taxicab bumper strips, radio broadcasts and spot announcements, sidewalk interviews, office meetings, shop and plant meetings, civic club engagements, school appointments, and many church service assignments brought the spiritual challenge to the people.

A chiropractor, Dr. Walter E. Sligh, led the crusade effort. Yeoman help came from insurance executive Don Kelso and realtor Ken Harris in particular. More than two hundred commitments of faith resulted from the nine-day lay efforts. More than fifty thousand persons had been left without excuse.

In March, the town of Union City, Tennessee, (9000), in Obion County just south of the Kentucky border, felt the impact of spiritual revival. Some twenty thousand people within the county's limits heard the Gospel message from Christian business and professional men. CBMCI Special Representative Reid Jepson directed the public program. It was, however, the three-year efforts of lay and pastoral personnel which paved the way for what followed.

General Chairman Robert McAdoo and the Reverend Dick Coons, pastor of Cumberland Presbyterian Church, captained the crusade team. Many others assisted, but these two bore the brunt of preparation.

When a Southern Bell telephone man came to install a second phone in crusade headquarters at the Davy Crockett Hotel, he asked if he might meet one of the speakers. The night before, while lying in bed at home alone, listening to the radio, he heard a business man testify of his faith before the crusade audience in the Union City High School gymnasium. When the speaker asked for commitments in the gymnasium and beside radios, the telephone repairman dropped to his knees in surrender to God. Now he wanted to thank the speaker personally.

An eighty-one-year-old lady wrote crusade headquarters expressing gratitude to God and thanks to the leaders for allowing her to witness a real "John and Charles Wesley revival" in her day. Some 1,750 persons attended the two meetings on Saturday night. The extra meeting was scheduled to handle overflow crowds. At the gymnasium, seventy inquirers, mostly young people, filled the counseling room. Tears flowed freely. Head Counselor Eugene Scheele, superintendent of the Holland (Michigan) Rescue Mission, called it the greatest manifestation of the Holy Spirit he had ever seen.

Veteran CBMC speakers said, "Fruit was ripe for the picking." Young and old alike had been softened by the three-year avalanche of prayer that had paved the way for a spiritual harvest.

Other crusades continued and reaped eternal results. A different kind of ministry provided six months of spiritual thrills on the West coast. A specially-constructed "Sermons from Science" building at Century 21 in Seattle housed scientific exhibit and display. Members of the CBMC of Seattle, led by Leonard Gustafson, supported the unusual ministry. Dr. George Speake of the Moody Institute of Science conducted the daily witness. Hundreds of commitments resulted. Alertness to opportunity continued to distinguish the lay movement.

CHAPTER TWENTY-FOUR

BUILDERS FOR ETERNITY

Isn't it strange that princes and kings,
And clowns that caper in sawdust rings,
And common people like you and me
Are builders for eternity?

-Selected

MAINTAINING A PROPER IMAGE has never been an easy undertaking for any organization. Christian Business Men's Committee is no exception. Among its fifteen thousand members in thirty-five countries are men of numerous denominations, vastly different cultural backgrounds, and widely divergent views on some matters. Ideally, however, CBMC has a primary aim and purpose, majoring in the essential of man-to-man witnessing.

Some pastors take a dim view of the movement until they learn firsthand what it is all about. If they will listen, and many do, they soon learn that CBMC is a "plus effort" for active church workers; a missionary arm in the professional and business world. Mealtime evangelism is a prime avenue of witness; many laymen attest to its effectiveness.

To counteract the anti-church charge sometimes leveled at CBMC, a committee took a poll. The poll showed that 100% of the committee members were active church members; 92% attended either morning or evening services; 67% were teachers, officers or superintendents of Sunday Schools; 76% attended prayer meetings; 63% were church officers, and 30% sang in church choirs. Many pastors affirm that their men are better church members for having associated with CBMC.

"I have seen CBMC function many times," a California pastor wrote. "Its members have been a source of real inspiration and challenge to me. I thank God there are men in our country who are ready to make known their uncompromising stand for Jesus Christ."

Dr. A. P. White, pastor of Beulah Baptist Church, Detroit, asserted: "Praise God for laymen able and willing to 'stand in the gap.' Let us not fail to pray for one another as the shadows lengthen, difficulties become more stupendous and the coming of our Lord draweth nigh."

Many other pastors have expressed approval of CBMC, not because it is faultless but because it aims to help the church. R. G. LeTourneau voiced the sentiments of many Christian leaders today, in and outside the CBMC movement.

"The most encouraging sign on the horizon today," he said, "is the fact that businessmen are waking up to their responsibility to God, and beginning to prove that Christianity is practical."

Projection of the first twenty-five years would indicate a continuation of the slow but steady growth of the movement. No longer an infant, or even an irrepressible teenager, Christian Business Men's Committee International bids fair to reach its potential in coming days.

From clerks to cooks, farmers to fishermen, bakers to bankers, lawyers to doctors, mayors to publishers, dedicated laymen – men aflame - continue to build for eternity.

To be continued

You are the future of the CBMC story.

The Lord values you, and every one chosen is significant in His sight. He is transforming you to reign with Him for all eternity. His work through your life on earth will prepare you for that role. Today, you are like an earthen vessel containing a valuable treasure, but in heaven you will be like purified gold, a magnificent work of art.

The stories in this book represent where your story began. Past leaders in CBMC have established a foundation of great treasure upon which you can continue to build in your own life, in your family's lives, and in the lives of businessmen around you. Through CBMC, you aren't investing in worldly things which will rust and perish. You are investing in eternal things, presenting yourself as a living sacrifice for the glory of Christ all of your days.

You Are A Man Aflame!

ABOUT THE AUTHOR OF THE ORIGINAL 1962 EDITION

DAVID R. ENLOW

David R. Enlow is director of publications for Christian Business Men's Committee International and also managing editor of its magazine *CBMC Contact* with officies in Chicago. He spent five years as a newspaperman with the *Orlando Sentinel-Star*, Orlando, Florida. He was a copy editor when he left the newspaper in the summer of 1951 to become managing editor of *Christian Life* magazine in Chicago. In August 1952, he began his work with CBMCI. Journalism has been a major interest since high school with further studies take at Wheaton College, the Armed Services Institute, and the Newspaper Institute of America.

Enlow teaches the Men's Bible Class at the Southwest Christian and Missionary Alliance Church in Chicago's suburban Oak Lawn area and is a member of the church board. He has spoken at various conferences, retreats, and rallies. He edits The Religious Caravan news page in The Alliance Witness, official publication of the Christian and Missionary Alliance, edited by Dr. A.W. Tozer.

Born in Orlando, Florida, he attended Wheaton College (1936-37).

Made in the USA
Lexington, KY
24 September 2019